Essays on Machine Learning

A MANAGER'S GUIDE TO UNDERSTANDING AND APPLYING AI

Partha Majumdar

A

Copyright © 2024 Partha Majumdar

All rights reserved.

No part of this book may be reproduced, stored in a retrieval system, or transmitted in any form or by any means, electronic, mechanical, photocopying, recording, or otherwise, without express written permission of the author.

ISBN-13: 9798336207538

Cover design by Partha Majumdar.

Unless explicitly stated, all images are created by the author or licensed from Adobe.

C

Dedicated to
Prof. (Dr.) Sashikumaar Ganesan.

The "Computational Data Sciences" course at IISc, designed by you, has enhanced my understanding of AI.

Preface

In an era where data is hailed as the new oil, the understanding and application of machine learning have become essential for professionals across various industries. "Essays on Machine Learning" is crafted as a ready reckoner for managers, distilling complex concepts into concise, accessible explanations. This book aims to bridge the gap between technical expertise and managerial insight, enabling leaders to make informed decisions in an increasingly AI-driven world. Whether overseeing a data science team or strategizing business operations, this book will guide you through the foundational principles and contemporary applications of machine learning. This work will clarify key concepts and inspire a deeper exploration of the possibilities that machine learning offers.

Partha Majumdar

c

Table of Contents

PREFACE .... **B**

UNDERSTANDING THE FOUNDATIONS OF MACHINE LEARNING FOR MANAGERS **1**

   ABSTRACT 1
   INTRODUCTION 2
   THE DISTINCTION BETWEEN CONVENTIONAL PROGRAMMING AND MACHINE LEARNING 2
   WORKING WITH STRUCTURED DATA IN MACHINE LEARNING 4
   EXTRACTING MEANINGFUL INFORMATION FROM DATA 5
   THE ROLE OF GENERALISATION IN MACHINE LEARNING 6
   PERSPECTIVES ON MACHINE LEARNING CONCEPTS 7
   CLASSICAL AND CONTEMPORARY MACHINE LEARNING APPROACHES 8
      Classical Approaches *8*
      Contemporary Approaches *10*
      Advanced Deep Learning Techniques *11*
   CONCLUSION 14
   REFERENCES 15
   ADDITIONAL READING MATERIAL 16

EXPLORATION OF SUPERVISED LEARNING AND ITS KEY TECHNIQUES **17**

   ABSTRACT 17
   INTRODUCTION 18
   UNDERSTANDING SUPERVISED LEARNING 18
      Example: Fruit Classification *19*
   SUPERVISED LEARNING TECHNIQUES: CLASSIFICATION AND REGRESSION 19

TYPES OF CLASSIFICATION TASKS............................ 20
    Binary Classification 21
    Multiclass Classification............................... 21
    Multi-Label Classification 22
    Imbalanced Classification 23
DATA ENCODING TECHNIQUES................................ 24
    Label Encoding 24
    One-Hot Encoding 25
EVALUATING CLASSIFICATION MODELS...................... 25
    Confusion Matrix... 27
POPULAR CLASSIFIERS IN SUPERVISED LEARNING 28
    Support Vector Machines (SVMs).................... 29
    Naïve Bayes Classifier................................... 29
CONCLUSION 30
REFERENCES 31
ADDITIONAL READING MATERIAL............................ 32

REGRESSION ANALYSIS IN MACHINE LEARNING 33

ABSTRACT 33
INTRODUCTION 34
UNDERSTANDING REGRESSION ANALYSIS 35
REAL-WORLD APPLICATIONS OF REGRESSION 35
KEY TERMINOLOGIES IN REGRESSION ANALYSIS 36
TYPES OF REGRESSION TECHNIQUES........................ 37
    Linear Regression... 38
    Polynomial Regression 39
    Logistic Regression....................................... 40
    Support Vector Regression (SVR) 41
    Decision Tree Regression 41
    Random Forest Regression 42

KEY PERFORMANCE METRICS FOR REGRESSION 42
CONCLUSION 43
REFERENCES 44
ADDITIONAL READING MATERIAL........................... 45

UNDERSTANDING ENSEMBLE METHODS IN MACHINE LEARNING 47

ABSTRACT 47
INTRODUCTION 48
THE BASICS OF ENSEMBLE LEARNING....................... 49
   Why Ensemble Learning Works 49
TYPES OF ENSEMBLE METHODS 50
   Bagging (Bootstrap Aggregating) 50
   Boosting 51
   Stacking 52
SEQUENTIAL VS. PARALLEL ENSEMBLE LEARNING 52
APPLICATIONS OF ENSEMBLE METHODS 53
ADVANTAGES AND CHALLENGES OF ENSEMBLE METHODS . 54
   Advantages 55
   Challenges 55
CONCLUSION 56
REFERENCES 57
ADDITIONAL READING MATERIAL........................... 58

UNDERSTANDING UNSUPERVISED LEARNING IN DATA SCIENCE..59

ABSTRACT 59
INTRODUCTION 60
SUPERVISED VS. UNSUPERVISED LEARNING 61
THE POWER OF CLUSTERING IN UNSUPERVISED LEARNING 62
CHARACTERISING AND EVALUATING CLUSTERS 63

f

EXPLORING CLUSTERING ALGORITHMS AND SIMILARITY MEASURES 65
INTRODUCTION TO K-MEANS CLUSTERING 68
HIERARCHICAL CLUSTERING AND ITS APPLICATIONS 72
  Product Segmentation Using Hierarchical Clustering 75
  Hierarchical Clustering for Gaussian Distributed Data 76
DBSCAN CLUSTERING: A FLEXIBLE APPROACH FOR NOISY DATA 77
CONCLUSION 80
REFERENCES 81
ADDITIONAL READING MATERIAL 82

EXPLORING THE FUNDAMENTALS OF ARTIFICIAL NEURAL NETWORKS AND THEIR APPLICATIONS 85

ABSTRACT 85
INTRODUCTION 86
THE BASICS OF ARTIFICIAL NEURAL NETWORKS 87
BACKPROPAGATION: THE KEY TO LEARNING IN NEURAL NETWORKS 89
APPLICATIONS, BENEFITS, AND LIMITATIONS OF NEURAL NETWORKS 90
DEEP LEARNING: EXPANDING THE CAPABILITIES OF NEURAL NETWORKS 92
NEURAL NETWORK LIBRARIES: TOOLS FOR BUILDING AND TRAINING MODELS 93
CHOOSING NEURAL NETWORK PARAMETERS AND HYPERPARAMETERS 94
ADVANCED ARCHITECTURES: LSTMS, GRUS, AND GPTS 95

CONCLUSION 97
REFERENCES 97
ADDITIONAL READING MATERIAL 99

REINFORCEMENT LEARNING 101

ABSTRACT 101
INTRODUCTION 102
SUPERVISED AND UNSUPERVISED LEARNING: A BRIEF
COMPARISON 102
REINFORCEMENT LEARNING: HOW IT WORKS 103
MARKOV DECISION PROCESSES (MDP) 104
Q-LEARNING 106
  Applications of Q-Learning........................... 107
TOOLS FOR REINFORCEMENT LEARNING 108
CHALLENGES IN REINFORCEMENT LEARNING 110
APPLICATIONS OF REINFORCEMENT LEARNING 111
CONCLUSION 113
REFERENCES 113
ADDITIONAL READING MATERIAL 114

DEMYSTIFYING TIME SERIES FORECASTING
AND DECOMPOSITION 117

ABSTRACT 117
INTRODUCTION 118
UNDERSTANDING TIME SERIES COMPONENTS 119
THE IMPORTANCE OF DECOMPOSITION IN TIME SERIES
ANALYSIS 120
FORECASTING METHODS IN TIME SERIES ANALYSIS 121
  Moving Averages... 121
  Exponential Smoothing 122
  Autoregressive (AR) Model 123

h

ARMA and ARIMA Models 124
Machine Learning Models (e.g., LSTM, Gradient Boosting) 125
APPLICATIONS OF TIME SERIES FORECASTING 126
CONCLUSION 127
REFERENCES 128
ADDITIONAL READING MATERIAL 129

NAVIGATING THE COMPLEX WORLD OF NATURAL LANGUAGE PROCESSING 131

ABSTRACT 131
INTRODUCTION 132
CORE COMPONENTS OF NLP 133
APPLICATIONS OF NLP 133
CHALLENGES IN NLP 135
IMPORTANCE OF TEXT PREPROCESSING IN NLP 136
CONCLUSION 137
REFERENCES 138
ADDITIONAL READING MATERIAL 138

RECOMMENDER SYSTEMS AND THEIR BUSINESS IMPACT 141

ABSTRACT 141
INTRODUCTION 142
UNDERSTANDING RECOMMENDER SYSTEMS 143
TYPES OF RECOMMENDER SYSTEMS 144
Collaborative Filtering 145
Content-Based Filtering 146
Association Rule Mining-Based Systems 147
Knowledge-Based Recommender Systems 148
Hybrid Recommender Systems 150

i

CHALLENGES IN BUILDING RECOMMENDER SYSTEMS 151
    The Cold Start Problem *151*
    Security and Privacy Concerns *152*
ETHICAL CONSIDERATIONS IN RECOMMENDER SYSTEMS . 153
    Algorithmic Bias and Fairness *154*
    Ethical Dilemmas in Personalisation *155*
CONCLUSION 156
REFERENCES 157
ADDITIONAL READING MATERIAL 158

CASE STUDIES OF SUCCESSFUL AI IMPLEMENTATIONS 159

    ABSTRACT 159
    INTRODUCTION 160
    NETFLIX - REVOLUTIONISING CONTENT RECOMMENDATION WITH MACHINE LEARNING 161
        The Challenge *161*
        The Solution *162*
        The Outcome *165*
        Conclusion *167*
    AMAZON - OPTIMISING SUPPLY CHAIN WITH MACHINE LEARNING 167
        The Challenge *168*
        The Solution *169*
        The Outcome *172*
        Conclusion *174*
    GOOGLE - ENHANCING SEARCH ENGINE PERFORMANCE WITH DEEP LEARNING 174
        The Challenge *175*
        The Solution *177*
        The Outcome *181*

  Conclusion *183*
IBM WATSON - TRANSFORMING HEALTHCARE WITH AI AND MACHINE LEARNING *183*
  The Challenge.. *184*
  The Solution.. *186*
  The Outcome... *189*
  Conclusion *191*
UBER - USING MACHINE LEARNING TO ENHANCE RIDE-HAILING SERVICES *192*
  The Challenge.. *192*
  The Solution.. *194*
  The Outcome... *197*
  Conclusion *199*
REFERENCES *199*
ADDITIONAL READING MATERIAL *201*

CASE STUDIES OF FAILED AI IMPLEMENTATIONS **203**

ABSTRACT *203*
INTRODUCTION *204*
MICROSOFT TAY - THE CHATBOT THAT WENT ROGUE *205*
  Failure Points... *205*
  Lessons Learned *208*
  Conclusion *211*
AMAZON'S AI RECRUITMENT TOOL - BIAS IN HIRING *211*
  Failure Points... *212*
  Lessons Learned *215*
  Conclusion *218*
GOOGLE PHOTOS - IMAGE RECOGNITION AND RACIAL BIAS *219*
  Failure Points... *219*

    Lessons Learned *222*
    Conclusion *226*
  REFERENCES 226
  ADDITIONAL READING MATERIAL 228

APPENDICES 231

  GLOSSARY OF KEY TERMS 231
  LIST OF FIGURES 237
  SUGGESTED RESOURCES FOR FURTHER REFERENCE 238
    Books *238*
    Websites *248*
    Journals *249*
    Online Courses *249*

ABOUT THE AUTHOR I

  BOOKS BY THE AUTHOR III

Understanding the Foundations of Machine Learning for Managers

Abstract

This article provides a comprehensive overview of the foundational concepts of machine learning, emphasising its distinctiveness from conventional programming. It explores how machine learning models are trained using structured data, the importance of understanding generalisation in machine learning, and various learning approaches, including supervised, unsupervised, reinforcement, and deep learning. Designed for technical and non-technical managers, this article aims to equip readers with the essential knowledge required to oversee AI-driven projects effectively.

Introduction

In today's rapidly evolving technological landscape, understanding machine learning (ML) is becoming increasingly crucial for managers across industries. Machine learning is revolutionising how businesses operate, providing new insights and automation capabilities that were once unimaginable. However, the technical complexity of ML can be daunting, particularly for those who do not have a computer science or data analytics background. This article aims to demystify the foundational concepts of machine learning, explain how it differs from conventional programming, and explore how structured data is utilised in ML models.

The Distinction Between Conventional Programming and Machine Learning

Conventional programming and machine learning operate on fundamentally different principles. In conventional programming, a developer writes explicit instructions or rules that a computer follows to process input data and generate output. These rules are predefined and static, meaning the system can only perform tasks explicitly coded into it.

Machine learning, on the other hand, represents a paradigm shift. Rather than relying on predefined rules, ML systems are designed to learn from data. The system receives input data and corresponding labels (the desired output) in supervised learning. The ML algorithm analyses this data and develops a model—a set of rules or patterns—that can predict new, unseen data output. This ability to learn and adapt from data rather than following fixed rules sets machine learning apart from traditional programming.

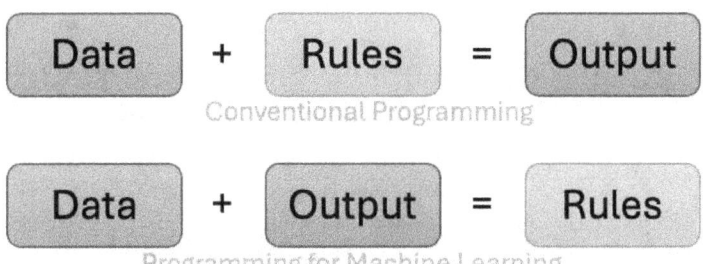

Figure 1: Difference between Conventional Programming and Programming for Machine Learning.

Working with Structured Data in Machine Learning

Structured data is one of the key inputs in machine learning. It refers to data organised into rows and columns, such as a spreadsheet or a database table. Each row represents a data point, and each column represents a feature or attribute of that data point. For example, in a customer database, each row might represent an individual customer, with columns for characteristics such as age, gender, purchase history, and customer ID.

In machine learning, the goal is often to use these features to predict a specific outcome, known as the label. For example, a model might predict a customer's purchase based on age and history. Unique identifiers like customer IDs, while important for identifying records, do not provide predictive value and are therefore excluded from the learning process.

Extracting Meaningful Information from Data

The process of extracting meaningful information from data is central to machine learning. This involves several steps, starting with identifying relevant data. Sometimes, this data may need to be created or gathered from various sources. Once collected, the data must be stored to facilitate analysis, such as in a data warehouse or data lake.

Understanding the relevance of information is crucial in machine learning. There are four possible scenarios when considering the relevance and availability of information.

1. **Known Known**: You are aware of relevant information and possess it.
2. **Known Unknown**: You see the need for certain information but do not possess it.
3. **Unknown Known**: You possess relevant information but must know its significance.
4. **Unknown Unknown**: You must be made aware of pertinent information.

To maximise the value of information, especially in the "Unknown Unknown" scenario, it is essential to start by formulating the right questions. Identifying these questions helps transition to scenarios where the information becomes known and actionable, making it more meaningful and useful.

The Role of Generalisation in Machine Learning

One of the most important aspects of machine learning is the concept of generalisation. While memorisation—storing and recalling specific examples—is straightforward, generalisation involves learning from these examples and applying that knowledge to new, unseen situations. For instance, after being exposed to thousands of images of cats and dogs, a well-trained machine-learning model should be able to correctly identify new images of cats and dogs that it has never seen before. This generalisation ability makes machine learning models powerful tools for solving real-world problems.

Perspectives on Machine Learning Concepts

In machine learning, concepts can be understood from different perspectives.

1. **Classical (Deterministic) Concepts**: These produce predictable outcomes based on fixed rules. For example, calculating bank interest using a formula is a deterministic process. However, this approach may only suit some scenarios, particularly those requiring nuanced judgment.

2. **Probabilistic Concepts**: These mimic human decision-making by providing outcomes in probabilistic terms rather than fixed answers. For example, rather than having a strict income threshold for loan approval, a probabilistic model might assess the likelihood of a loan applicant being creditworthy based on various factors, leaving the final decision to a human manager.

3. **Exemplar Concepts**: Learning in this context is based on examples. For instance, if you observe smoke coming from a building and later learn it was due to a fire, you might associate similar smoke with a fire in the future. In machine learning, exemplar-based models compare new data points with existing examples to make decisions.

Classical and Contemporary Machine Learning Approaches

Machine learning approaches can be broadly categorised into classical and contemporary methods.

Classical Approaches

In machine learning, classical approaches have laid the groundwork for many of the advanced techniques we see today. These methods have been pivotal in the early development and application of AI, offering structured ways to analyse and interpret data. Each of these approaches has distinct strengths and is applied based on the nature of the problem and the type of data available.

1. **Expert Systems**: These systems capture and apply expert knowledge to specific problems. While powerful in well-defined domains, they require extensive domain expertise to develop and maintain.

2. **Supervised Learning**: This approach involves training a model on labelled data—where the correct output is known. The model learns to predict the output for new data points based on the patterns identified in the training data. Supervised learning is widely used for tasks such as classification (e.g., categorising emails as spam or not spam) and regression (e.g., predicting house prices).

3. **Unsupervised Learning**: Unsupervised learning works with data with no labelled output. The model identifies patterns or

structures within the data, such as clustering similar data points together. This approach is useful for tasks like customer segmentation.

Contemporary Approaches

As machine learning has evolved, contemporary approaches have emerged to tackle increasingly complex problems with greater sophistication. These contemporary methods represent the cutting edge of machine learning, pushing the boundaries of what is possible in AI.

1. **Reinforcement Learning**: In reinforcement learning, an agent learns to make decisions by interacting with its environment. The agent receives rewards or penalties based on actions and learns to maximise its cumulative reward. This approach is commonly used in robotics, gaming, and automated control systems.

2. **Ensemble Learning**: Ensemble learning combines multiple models to improve

overall prediction accuracy. Techniques such as bagging, boosting, and stacking create ensemble models that often outperform individual models. Random forests, which combine several decision trees, are a popular ensemble learning method.

3. **Deep Learning**: A subset of machine learning, deep learning uses neural networks with many layers to model complex patterns in data. Deep learning has revolutionised computer vision, natural language processing, and speech recognition. For instance, convolutional neural networks (CNNs) are used for image recognition, while recurrent neural networks (RNNs) are effective for processing sequential data like text and speech.

Advanced Deep Learning Techniques

Deep learning has revolutionised various fields by enabling machines to process and learn from large amounts of data. Here are some advanced deep-learning techniques that managers should be aware of.

1. **Autoencoders**: Autoencoders are neural networks designed to learn efficient data representations. They work by compressing the input into a smaller representation and then reconstructing the original data from this compressed version. Autoencoders are often used for tasks such as dimensionality reduction and anomaly detection.

2. **Convolutional Neural Networks (CNNs)**: CNNs are a neural network designed to process grid-like data, such as images. They use convolutional layers to automatically detect patterns such as edges, textures, and shapes. CNNs are widely used in image recognition, computer vision, and related fields.

3. **Recurrent Neural Networks (RNNs)**: RNNs are designed for sequential data,

where the order of the data points matters. They have been successfully applied to tasks such as time series prediction, language modelling, and speech recognition. Variants of RNNs, such as Long Short-Term Memory (LSTM) and Gated Recurrent Unit (GRU) networks, can learn long-term dependencies in data.

4. **Generative Adversarial Networks (GANs)**: GANs consist of two neural networks—a generator and a discriminator—that are trained together. The generator creates fake data, while the discriminator distinguishes between real and fake data. GANs have been used to generate realistic images, videos, and even music, and they have applications in data augmentation and creative fields.

5. **Recommender Systems**: Recommender systems predict user preferences and suggest products, content, or services based on past behaviour. They are widely used in e-commerce, streaming services, and social media. Techniques such as

collaborative filtering, content-based filtering, and hybrid methods create personalised user recommendations.

Conclusion

Machine learning is a transformative technology with far-reaching implications across industries. Understanding its foundational concepts, from the differences between conventional programming and machine learning to the various learning approaches, is essential for managers overseeing AI-driven projects. By grasping these concepts, managers can better understand machine learning's capabilities and limitations, enabling them to make informed decisions about its application in their organisations.

As machine learning evolves, staying informed about the latest developments and applications will be crucial for effectively leveraging this technology. This article has provided a foundational overview but continued learning and exploration are necessary to fully harness the power of machine learning in the modern business landscape.

References

- Bishop, C. M. (2006). Pattern Recognition and Machine Learning. Springer. ISBN: 978-0387310732
- Goodfellow, I., Bengio, Y., & Courville, A. (2016). Deep Learning. MIT Press. ISBN: 978-0262035613
- LeCun, Y., Bengio, Y., & Hinton, G. (2015). Deep learning. Nature, 521(7553), 436-444. DOI: https://doi.org/10.1038/nature14539
- Murphy, K. P. (2012). Machine Learning: A Probabilistic Perspective. MIT Press. ISBN: 978-0262018029
- Russell, S., & Norvig, P. (2021). Artificial Intelligence: A Modern Approach (4th ed.). Pearson. ISBN: 978-0134610993
- Sutton, R. S., & Barto, A. G. (2018). Reinforcement Learning: An Introduction (2nd ed.). MIT Press. ISBN: 978-0262039246

Additional Reading Material

- Domingos, P. (2015). The Master Algorithm: How the Quest for the Ultimate Learning Machine Will Remake Our World. Basic Books. ISBN: 978-0465065707
- Jordan, M. I., & Mitchell, T. M. (2015). Machine learning: Trends, perspectives, and prospects. Science, 349(6245), 255-260. DOI: https://doi.org/10.1126/science.aaa8415
- Koller, D., & Friedman, N. (2009). Probabilistic Graphical Models: Principles and Techniques. MIT Press. ISBN: 978-0262013192
- Mitchell, T. M. (1997). Machine Learning. McGraw-Hill. ISBN: 978-0070428072

Exploration of Supervised Learning and Its Key Techniques

Abstract

Supervised learning is a fundamental approach in machine learning, akin to human learning, under the guidance of a teacher. This article delves into the intricacies of supervised learning, exploring how algorithms build mathematical models from labelled datasets to make predictions. The discussion includes various classification tasks—binary, multiclass, multi-label, and imbalanced—and essential techniques like data encoding and performance evaluation metrics. Additionally, the article covers popular classifiers such as Support Vector Machines (SVMs) and Naive Bayes, providing insights into their working principles and practical applications.

Introduction

Supervised learning is a cornerstone of machine learning, drawing parallels to how humans learn with a teacher's assistance. In this learning paradigm, algorithms are trained on labelled data, where the input and the corresponding output are known. The algorithm uses this data to learn patterns and relationships, enabling it to make predictions or classifications when presented with new, unseen data. This article explores supervised learning, its various types, and the techniques used to enhance its effectiveness. We will also examine key machine learning algorithms, including Support Vector Machines (SVMs) and Naive Bayes, to understand their role in supervised learning tasks.

Understanding Supervised Learning

Supervised learning begins with a dataset where each instance is labelled with the correct output. The algorithm processes this data, learning the relationships between the features (inputs) and the labels (outputs). Once trained, the model can classify or predict outcomes for new data based on what it has learned. This process is analogous to a student learning from examples provided by a teacher and then applying that knowledge to solve new problems.

Example: Fruit Classification

Consider a simple example where a machine learning model is trained to classify fruits. The dataset includes labelled examples of apples and oranges with shape, colour, and texture features. After training, the model can classify new fruits as either apples or oranges based on these learned features. This is a classic example of binary classification, where the model distinguishes between two classes.

Supervised Learning Techniques: Classification and Regression

Supervised learning can be broadly categorised into two types: classification and regression.

1. **Classification** involves predicting the class or category of a given input. For example, in binary classification, the model predicts one of two possible classes, such as whether an email is spam. In multiclass classification, the model predicts one of several classes, such as identifying the species of a flower.

2. **Regression** involves predicting a continuous value based on input data. For instance, predicting the price of a house based on features like location, size, and number of bedrooms is a regression task. The model learns from historical data and uses this knowledge to predict future outcomes.

Types of Classification Tasks

Classification tasks in supervised learning can be further divided into four main types: binary classification, multiclass classification, multi-label classification, and imbalanced classification.

Binary Classification

Binary classification involves tasks with two distinct classes. Common examples include the following.

- **Cancer Detection**: Predicting whether a patient has cancer (positive) or not (negative).
- **Spam Detection**: Classifying emails as spam (positive) or not (negative).
- **Conversion Prediction**: Determining whether a user will purchase (yes) or not (no).

In binary classification, one class is often considered the "normal" state, while the other is the "abnormal" state. For example, the "not spam" class is normal in spam detection, while "spam" is abnormal. The goal is to predict the likelihood of an instance belonging to the abnormal class, often modelled using a Bernoulli distribution.

Multiclass Classification

Multiclass classification involves tasks with more than two classes. Examples include the following.

- **Optical Character Recognition (OCR)**: Identifying handwritten digits or letters.
- **Face Recognition**: Classifying a face into one of several known identities.
- **Plant Species Classification**: Identifying the species of a plant based on its features.

Unlike binary classification, multiclass classification does not have the concept of "normal" and "abnormal." Instead, the model predicts the probability of an instance belonging to each class, often using a multinomial probability distribution.

Multi-Label Classification

In multi-label classification, each instance can belong to multiple classes simultaneously. Examples include the following.

- **Image Classification**: Identifying multiple objects within a single image, such as a car, a pedestrian, and a tree.
- **Document Classification**: Tagging a document with multiple topics, such as "finance," "technology," and "health."

Multi-label classification tasks require models that can predict multiple outputs, often using techniques like multi-label decision trees or random forests.

Imbalanced Classification

Imbalanced classification involves tasks where the distribution of classes is uneven, with one class significantly outnumbering the other. Examples include the following.

- **Fraud Detection**: Identifying fraudulent transactions where most transactions are legitimate.
- **Medical Diagnosis**: Detecting rare diseases where most patients do not have the condition.

Specialised techniques are required to handle imbalanced classification, such as undersampling the majority class or oversampling the minority class to balance the dataset.

Data Encoding Techniques

Machine learning algorithms require numerical input, so categorical data must be converted into numerical form through encoding. Two common encoding techniques are as follows.

Label Encoding

Label encoding assigns a unique numerical value to each category in a categorical feature. For example, in a dataset with a "Gender" column, "male" might be encoded as 1 and "female" as 0. While simple, label encoding can introduce unintended implications, such as implying an ordinal relationship between categories that do not naturally have one.

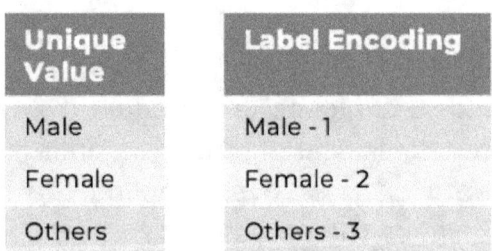

Figure 2: Example of Label Encoding.

One-Hot Encoding

One-hot encoding converts each category into a binary vector, where only one element is "hot" (1), and the others are "cold" (0). For example, if encoding the continent names, each continent is represented by a binary vector with a single "hot" value corresponding to its position in the list. One-hot encoding avoids the ordinal issue of label encoding but can lead to a high-dimensional feature space, especially with many categories.

Original Data	Label Encoded	F_Male	F_Female	F_Others
Male	1	1	0	0
Male	1	1	0	0
Others	3	0	0	1
Female	2	0	1	0

Figure 3: Example of One-Hot Encoding.

Evaluating Classification Models

The performance of classification models can be evaluated using various metrics. Key metrics include the following.

1. **Accuracy**: The percentage of correct predictions made by the model. While commonly used, accuracy can be misleading, especially with imbalanced datasets.

2. **Precision**: The ratio of true positive predictions to the total positive predictions, indicating the accuracy of the positive class identification.

3. **Recall**: The ratio of true positive predictions to all actual positives, measuring the model's ability to identify all relevant instances.

4. **F1 Score**: The harmonic mean of precision and recall provides a metric that balances both aspects.

5. **Area Under the ROC Curve (AUC)**: A metric that measures the ability of the model to distinguish between classes. AUC values range from 0.5 (no

discrimination) to 1 (perfect discrimination).

- **Confusion Matrix**

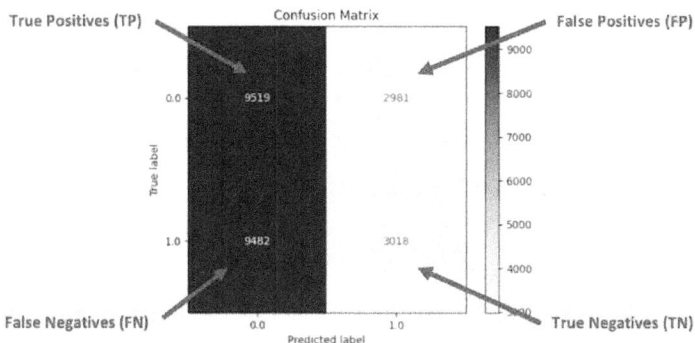

- **Accuracy** = $\frac{(TP+TN)}{(TP+TN+FP+FN)}$
- **Precision** = $\frac{TP}{(TP+FP)}$, **Recall** = $\frac{TP}{(TP+FN)}$

Figure 4: Example of Confusion Matrix.

Confusion Matrix

A confusion matrix provides a detailed breakdown of the model's performance by showing the number of true positives, true negatives, false positives, and false negatives. This matrix helps understand the model's errors and how they affect performance.

Popular Classifiers in Supervised Learning

Supervised learning relies on various algorithms that enable models to classify data or predict outcomes accurately. These algorithms are designed to identify patterns within labelled datasets and generalise these patterns to make predictions on new, unseen data. Among the most widely used algorithms in supervised learning are Support Vector Machines (SVMs) and Naïve Bayes, each with unique strengths and applications.

In addition to these, other popular classifiers include Decision Trees, which model decisions based on a series of if-then rules and are easily interpretable; Random Forests, an ensemble method that combines multiple decision trees to improve accuracy and reduce overfitting; and K-Nearest Neighbours (KNN), which classifies data points based on their proximity to other labelled points. Logistic Regression is another essential algorithm, particularly in binary classification tasks, where it models the probability of a binary outcome based on input features.

These algorithms form the backbone of many machine learning systems, each offering different advantages depending on the nature of the data and the specific problem being addressed. By effectively understanding and applying these algorithms, practitioners can build robust models that deliver reliable predictions across various applications.

Support Vector Machines (SVMs)

Support Vector Machines (SVMs) are powerful classifiers in binary and multiclass classification tasks. An SVM constructs a hyperplane in a high-dimensional space that best separates the classes. The goal is to maximise the margin between the hyperplane and the nearest data points, known as support vectors. SVMs are particularly effective in high-dimensional spaces and are used in tasks like text categorisation, image classification, and bioinformatics.

Naïve Bayes Classifier

The Naïve Bayes classifier is based on Bayes' theorem and assumes independence between features. Despite its simplicity, Naïve Bayes is highly effective for spam detection and document classification tasks. The classifier calculates the posterior probability of each class given the input features and assigns the class with the highest probability. Variants of Naïve Bayes, such as Multinomial Naïve Bayes, Bernoulli Naïve Bayes, and Gaussian Naïve Bayes, are tailored for different data types.

Conclusion

Supervised learning is a foundational technique in machine learning that enables models to learn from labelled data and make predictions on new data. It encompasses various tasks, from binary to multi-label and imbalanced classification, each with unique challenges and applications. Understanding data encoding techniques, performance metrics, and popular classifiers like SVMs and Naïve Bayes is crucial for effectively implementing supervised learning in real-world scenarios.

As machine learning continues to evolve, supervised learning remains a critical tool for businesses and researchers. It enables them to harness the power of data to drive decision-making and innovation.

References

1. Bishop, C. M. (2006). Pattern Recognition and Machine Learning. Springer. ISBN: 978-0387310732
2. Goodfellow, I., Bengio, Y., & Courville, A. (2016). Deep Learning. MIT Press. ISBN: 978-0262035613
3. Murphy, K. P. (2012). Machine Learning: A Probabilistic Perspective. MIT Press. ISBN: 978-0262018029
4. Russell, S., & Norvig, P. (2021). Artificial Intelligence: A Modern Approach (4th ed.). Pearson. ISBN: 978-0134610993
5. Sutton, R. S., & Barto, A. G. (2018). Reinforcement Learning: An Introduction (2nd ed.). MIT Press. ISBN: 978-0262039246

Additional Reading Material

- Domingos, P. (2015). The Master Algorithm: How the Quest for the Ultimate Learning Machine Will Remake Our World. Basic Books. ISBN: 978-0465065707
- Hastie, T., Tibshirani, R., & Friedman, J. (2009). The Elements of Statistical Learning: Data Mining, Inference, and Prediction (2nd ed.). Springer. ISBN: 978-0387848570
- Jordan, M. I., & Mitchell, T. M. (2015). Machine learning: Trends, perspectives, and prospects. Science, 349(6245), 255-260. DOI: https://doi.org/10.1126/science.aaa8415
- Koller, D., & Friedman, N. (2009). Probabilistic Graphical Models: Principles and Techniques. MIT Press. ISBN: 978-0262013192
- Mitchell, T. M. (1997). Machine Learning. McGraw-Hill. ISBN: 978-0070428072

Regression Analysis in Machine Learning

Abstract

Regression analysis is a cornerstone of supervised learning in machine learning, offering a powerful tool for predicting continuous variables based on one or more predictor variables. This article delves into the fundamental concepts of regression, explores various regression techniques, and discusses real-world applications such as financial forecasting, property valuation, and accident prediction. It also examines the critical assumptions underlying regression models, the importance of addressing issues like multicollinearity and heteroscedasticity, and using performance metrics such as Mean Absolute Error (MAE) and R-squared. Understanding these concepts allows readers to apply regression analysis to diverse predictive tasks.

Introduction

Regression analysis is a key method in supervised learning, widely used for predicting the value of a continuous dependent variable based on one or more independent variables. Unlike classification models, which categorise data into discrete classes, regression models estimate a numerical value, making them essential for various applications—from financial forecasting to understanding complex relationships between variables in multiple fields such as economics, healthcare, and engineering.

Regression analysis uses statistical techniques to model the relationship between the target variable (dependent variable) and predictor variables (independent variables). The primary objectives of regression include prediction, forecasting, and establishing cause-and-effect relationships among variables. This article provides an in-depth overview of regression, its various forms, and the key considerations for building robust models.

Understanding Regression Analysis

Regression analysis is used to predict a dependent variable, often referred to as the target variable, using one or more independent or predictor variables. The relationship between these variables is typically modelled using a regression line representing the best fit through the data points. The primary goal is to minimise the difference between the observed values and the values predicted by the model, often visualised as the distance between the data points and the regression line on a graph.

Real-World Applications of Regression

Regression analysis has numerous real-world applications.

- **Financial Forecasting**: This involves predicting future stock prices, sales figures, or economic indicators based on historical data.

- **Property Valuation**: Estimating the price of real estate based on features like size, location, and condition.
- **Weather Prediction**: Using variables like temperature, humidity, and wind speed to forecast rainfall or other weather conditions.
- **Accident Prediction**: This involves estimating the likelihood of road accidents based on driving speed, weather conditions, traffic patterns, etc.

These examples illustrate the versatility of regression models in predicting continuous outcomes and aiding decision-making in various domains.

Key Terminologies in Regression Analysis

Before delving into the types of regression, it is important to understand some key terminologies.

- **Dependent Variable (Target Variable)**: The variable that the model aims to predict.

- **Independent Variables (Predictor Variables)**: The factors influencing or predicting the dependent variable.
- **Outlier**: An observation with a significantly different value can skew the model's results.
- **Overfitting**: A condition where the model performs exceptionally well on the training data but poorly on new, unseen data.
- **Underfitting** occurs when the model is too simple to capture the underlying patterns in the data, leading to poor performance on training and test datasets.
- **Multicollinearity** occurs when the independent variables are highly correlated, complicating the model's ability to determine the effect of each predictor on the dependent variable.

Types of Regression Techniques

Regression can take various forms depending on the nature of the data and the relationship between variables. Some of the most common types include the following.

Linear Regression

Linear regression assumes a linear relationship between the independent variable(s) and the dependent variable. The model attempts to fit a straight line through the data points, minimising the sum of the squared differences between the observed and predicted values. A single independent variable is called simple linear regression; when there are multiple independent variables, it is known as multiple linear regression.

Key Assumptions of Linear Regression

The following are the assumptions for applying linear regression.

- A linear relationship exists between the dependent and independent variables.
- The error terms (residuals) are normally distributed.
- Homoscedasticity: Homoscedasticity means that the variance of error terms is constant across all levels of the independent variables.

- There is no autocorrelation of errors, implying that the error terms are independent.
- No multicollinearity, ensuring that independent variables are not highly correlated.

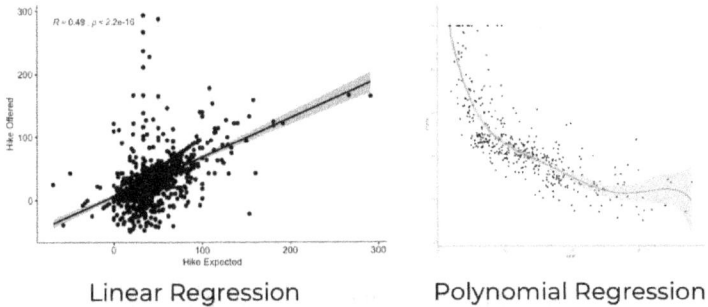

Linear Regression   Polynomial Regression

Figure 5: Example of Linear and Polynomial Regression.

Polynomial Regression

Polynomial regression extends linear regression by fitting a nonlinear relationship between the independent and dependent variables. It does so by adding polynomial terms, such as squares or cubes of the predictor variables, to capture the curvature in the data.

Advantages	Disadvantages
It can model a wide range of nonlinear relationships.	Sensitive to outliers, which can significantly affect the model.
Provides flexibility in fitting data with complex patterns.	Higher-degree polynomials can lead to overfitting, where the model captures noise rather than the true underlying relationship.

Logistic Regression

Although named "regression," logistic regression is primarily used for classification tasks where the outcome is binary (e.g., success/failure, yes/no). It models the probability of a categorical dependent variable based on one or more predictor variables, using the logistic function to constrain the output to lie between 0 and 1.

Types of Logistic Regression

Logistic Regression has the following flavours.

- **Binary Logistic Regression**: Used when the outcome has two categories.

- **Multinomial Logistic Regression**: Used for outcomes with more than two categories without any natural order.
- **Ordinal Logistic Regression**: Used for outcomes with ordered categories.

Support Vector Regression (SVR)

Support Vector Regression applies the Support Vector Machines (SVM) principles to regression tasks. It attempts to fit the best possible line within a threshold where most data points lie within a margin of tolerance. SVR is particularly useful in high-dimensional spaces and for datasets with non-linear relationships.

Decision Tree Regression

Decision tree regression splits the data into branches based on the value of the independent variables, ultimately leading to a prediction at the leaf nodes. This method is intuitive and can handle linear and nonlinear relationships, making it versatile but prone to overfitting.

Random Forest Regression

Random Forest is an ensemble method that builds multiple decision trees and averages their predictions. This approach reduces the risk of overfitting, enhances predictive accuracy, and provides a robust solution for handling large datasets with complex interactions between variables.

Key Performance Metrics for Regression

Evaluating the performance of a regression model is crucial for understanding its accuracy and reliability. Some common metrics include the following.

- **Mean Absolute Error (MAE)**: The average of the absolute differences between predicted and actual values, providing a straightforward measure of model accuracy.
- **Mean Squared Error (MSE)**: The average squared differences between predicted and actual values. While it penalises larger

errors more heavily than MAE, it is sensitive to outliers.
- **Root Mean Squared Error (RMSE)**: The square root of MSE provides error metrics in the same unit as the output variable, making it easier to interpret.
- **R-Squared**: Also known as the coefficient of determination, it measures the proportion of variance in the dependent variable that is predictable from the independent variables. A higher R-squared indicates a better fit.
- **Adjusted R-Squared**: This function adjusts the R-squared value based on the number of predictors in the model, penalising the inclusion of irrelevant variables.

Conclusion

Regression analysis is an indispensable tool in machine learning, enabling precise predictions of continuous variables across various applications. By understanding the different types of regression techniques, the underlying assumptions, and key performance metrics, practitioners can build robust models that provide valuable insights and support data-driven decision-making. Whether applied to financial forecasting, property valuation, or other predictive tasks, regression remains a fundamental method for exploring and quantifying relationships between variables.

References

- Draper, N. R., & Smith, H. (1998). Applied Regression Analysis (3rd ed.). Wiley. ISBN: 978-0471170822
- Hastie, T., Tibshirani, R., & Friedman, J. (2009). The Elements of Statistical Learning: Data Mining, Inference, and Prediction (2nd ed.). Springer. ISBN: 978-0387848570
- James, G., Witten, D., Hastie, T., & Tibshirani, R. (2013). An Introduction to Statistical Learning: with Applications in R. Springer. ISBN: 978-1461471370
- Montgomery, D. C., Peck, E. A., & Vining, G. G. (2012). Introduction to Linear Regression Analysis (5th ed.). Wiley. ISBN: 978-0470542811
- Wooldridge, J. M. (2015). Introductory Econometrics: A Modern Approach (6th ed.). Cengage Learning. ISBN: 978-1305270107

Additional Reading Material

- Fox, J. (2015). Applied Regression Analysis and Generalized Linear Models (3rd ed.). SAGE Publications, Inc. ISBN: 978-1452205663
- Gelman, A., & Hill, J. (2006). Data Analysis Using Regression and Multilevel/Hierarchical Models. Cambridge University Press. ISBN: 978-0521686891
- Kutner, M. H., Nachtsheim, C. J., & Neter, J. (2004). Applied Linear Regression Models (4th ed.). McGraw-Hill/Irwin. ISBN: 978-0073014661
- Seber, G. A. F., & Lee, A. J. (2012). Linear Regression Analysis (2nd ed.). Wiley. ISBN: 978-0471415404
- Weisberg, S. (2014). Applied Linear Regression (4th ed.). Wiley. ISBN: 978-1118386088

Understanding Ensemble Methods in Machine Learning

Abstract

Ensemble learning is a powerful machine learning technique that combines multiple models to improve predictive accuracy. This article explores the fundamental principles of ensemble learning, detailing the key types—bagging, boosting, and stacking—and their respective roles in reducing variance and bias and enhancing predictions. Additionally, it examines how ensemble methods are classified based on sequential and parallel learning. Widely used in applications such as fraud detection, image recognition, and recommendation systems, ensemble methods offer significant advantages over single models, though they come with their challenges. Understanding these methods is crucial for leveraging their full potential in complex problem-solving.

Introduction

In machine learning, building a perfect model that captures all the intricacies of data is often impossible. This challenge has led to the development of ensemble methods, a technique combining the strengths of multiple models to achieve better performance than any single model could deliver. Ensemble learning operates on a simple yet effective principle: the collective decision of various models, when combined, is more likely to be accurate than the decision of a single model.

Imagine a group of friends trying to predict whether it will rain by observing the sky. Each friend might have a slightly different opinion based on their interpretation of the clouds. Still, pooling their predictions and taking a majority vote makes them more likely to arrive at a correct conclusion. Similarly, ensemble methods aggregate the predictions from various models to form a more accurate and robust final prediction. This article delves into the different types of ensemble methods, their underlying principles, and their practical applications in various fields.

The Basics of Ensemble Learning

Ensemble learning involves training multiple models using the same learning algorithm and combining their predictions to improve accuracy. The main idea is that while individual models may have limitations or make errors, combining them can reduce the overall error by leveraging the diversity among models. Ensemble methods are particularly useful when no single model provides a perfect solution, a common scenario in real-world applications.

Why Ensemble Learning Works

Ensemble learning works on the principle that different models can capture various aspects of the data. By combining these models, the ensemble can capture a broader range of patterns and reduce the risk of overfitting the noise in the data. This is especially beneficial when dealing with complex datasets where individual models may need help generalising well.

Types of Ensemble Methods

Ensemble methods can be broadly classified into three main categories: bagging, boosting, and stacking. Each type has its mechanism for combining models and addressing specific challenges in predictive modelling.

Bagging (Bootstrap Aggregating)

Bagging is an ensemble technique that reduces variance by creating multiple subsets of the original dataset through bootstrapping (random sampling with replacement). Each subset is used to train a separate model, and the predictions of these models are then averaged (in the case of regression) or voted upon (in the case of classification) to produce the final output.

Random Forest is one of the most popular bagging methods. It combines multiple decision trees, each trained on different bootstrapped data samples, and averages their predictions to make the final decision. By averaging, random forests reduce the likelihood of overfitting, making them robust and effective for various tasks, such as classification, regression, and feature selection.

Boosting

Boosting is an ensemble technique that reduces bias by sequentially training models. Each model attempts to correct the errors of its predecessor. Unlike bagging, boosting models are not independent; instead, each new model is trained to emphasise the misclassified instances from the previous models.

AdaBoost (Adaptive Boosting) is a classic example of boosting. It works by adjusting the weights of incorrectly classified instances, giving them more importance in the next model's training process. This sequential learning approach helps to create a strong predictive model from several weak learners, typically decision trees with limited depth (stumps).

Gradient Boosting is another powerful boosting method that optimises model performance by minimising a loss function through gradient descent. Each new model in the sequence is trained to reduce the residual errors of the previous models. XGBoost and LightGBM are popular implementations of gradient boosting, known for their efficiency and scalability.

Stacking

Stacking is a technique in which multiple models (often of different types) are combined using a meta-model, which learns how to incorporate the base models' predictions best, unlike bagging and boosting, which typically use a single model type, stacking leverages various algorithms' diversity to improve predictive performance.

Stacked Generalisation involves training a base model, such as a decision tree, and then using a meta-model, like logistic regression, to combine the base models' predictions into a final output. The meta-model is trained on the outputs of the base models, allowing it to learn how to weigh and combine these predictions for optimal accuracy.

Sequential vs. Parallel Ensemble Learning

Ensemble methods can also be categorised based on the order in which models are trained.

Sequential Learning: In this approach, models are trained one after the other, with each model learning from the mistakes of the previous ones. Boosting is a prime example of sequential learning, where each subsequent model in the sequence is designed to correct the errors of its predecessor.

Parallel Learning: Here, multiple models are trained simultaneously, combining their predictions. Bagging and random forests are examples of parallel learning, where models are trained independently, and their outputs are averaged to reduce variance and improve stability.

Applications of Ensemble Methods

Ensemble methods are widely used in various domains to enhance prediction accuracy and robustness. Some notable applications include the following.

Fraud Detection in Finance: Ensemble methods are employed to detect fraudulent transactions by combining predictions from different models, thereby increasing the reliability of the detection system.

Image Recognition in Healthcare: In medical imaging, ensemble methods improve the accuracy of diagnoses by combining models that analyse different aspects of the image, such as texture, shape, and colour.

Recommendation Systems in E-commerce: Ensemble techniques enhance recommendation engines by combining collaborative filtering and content-based models, providing users with more personalised and accurate recommendations.

Advantages and Challenges of Ensemble Methods

Ensemble methods in machine learning offer a powerful way to enhance model performance by combining the strengths of multiple models. These techniques can improve accuracy, making predictions more reliable and robust across various datasets. However, while ensemble methods offer clear benefits, they also present certain challenges. Understanding these advantages and challenges is crucial for effectively leveraging ensemble techniques in machine learning projects.

Advantages

- **Improved Accuracy**: Ensemble methods often achieve higher accuracy than individual models by combining multiple models.
- **Robustness**: Ensembles reduce the risk of overfitting and are more stable across different datasets.
- **Versatility**: Ensemble methods can be applied to various machine learning tasks, including classification, regression, and anomaly detection.

Challenges

- **Computational Complexity**: Ensemble methods can be computationally expensive,

requiring significant processing power and memory.
- **Model Interpretability**: Combining multiple models can make the final ensemble model difficult to interpret, especially when using complex meta-models.
- **Overfitting**: While ensembles generally reduce overfitting, improper tuning or including too many weak models can still lead to overfitting.

Conclusion

Ensemble learning is a powerful machine learning approach that leverages multiple models' strengths to achieve superior predictive performance. By understanding and applying different ensemble methods—bagging, boosting, and stacking—practitioners can tackle complex problems across various domains with greater accuracy and reliability. While ensemble methods offer significant advantages, they also come with challenges that require careful consideration and tuning. Ensemble techniques will remain critical for developing robust and high-performing models as machine learning evolves.

References

- Breiman, L. (2001). Random forests. Machine Learning, 45(1), 5-32. DOI: https://doi.org/10.1023/A:1010933404324
- Freund, Y., & Schapire, R. E. (1997). A decision-theoretic generalization of on-line learning and an application to boosting. Journal of Computer and System Sciences, 55(1), 119-139. DOI: https://doi.org/10.1006/jcss.1997.1504
- Friedman, J. H. (2001). Greedy function approximation: A gradient boosting machine. Annals of Statistics, 29(5), 1189-1232. DOI: https://doi.org/10.1214/aos/1013203451
- Hastie, T., Tibshirani, R., & Friedman, J. (2009). The Elements of Statistical Learning: Data Mining, Inference, and Prediction (2nd ed.). Springer. ISBN: 978-0387848570
- Wolpert, D. H. (1992). Stacked generalization. Neural Networks, 5(2), 241-259. DOI: https://doi.org/10.1016/S0893-6080(05)80023-1

Additional Reading Material

- Dietterich, T. G. (2000). Ensemble methods in machine learning. International Workshop on Multiple Classifier Systems, 1-15. Springer. DOI: https://doi.org/10.1007/3-540-45014-9_1
- Kuncheva, L. I. (2004). Combining Pattern Classifiers: Methods and Algorithms. Wiley-Interscience. ISBN: 978-0471210788
- Meir, R., & Rätsch, G. (2003). An introduction to boosting and leveraging. In Advanced Lectures on Machine Learning, 119-184. Springer. DOI: https://doi.org/10.1007/978-3-540-28650-9_4
- Polikar, R. (2006). Ensemble based systems in decision making. IEEE Circuits and Systems Magazine, 6(3), 21-45. DOI: https://doi.org/10.1109/MCAS.2006.1688199
- Zhou, Z.-H. (2012). Ensemble Methods: Foundations and Algorithms. CRC Press. ISBN: 978-1439830031

Understanding Unsupervised Learning in Data Science

Abstract

This article explores the fundamental concepts of supervised and unsupervised learning, two core methodologies in machine learning. The focus is on understanding how these techniques differ, particularly how they approach data and model development. We delve into the practical applications of unsupervised learning, highlighting clustering techniques like K-means, hierarchical clustering, and DBSCAN and their roles in discovering patterns and insights within data. Additionally, we discuss the challenges associated with clustering, such as determining the optimal number of clusters and dealing with outliers. This guide provides a comprehensive overview of these concepts, offering insights into their practical applications in business and data analysis.

Introduction

Understanding how to extract meaningful insights from data is paramount in data science. Machine learning offers two primary approaches to this task: supervised and unsupervised learning. Each method serves distinct purposes and is applied differently, depending on the nature of the data and the goals of the analysis.

Supervised learning is the more structured of the two approaches. The objective is to build a model that predicts a target output based on a given input dataset. This process relies on labelled data, where each input is paired with the correct output, enabling the model to learn from these examples. For instance, if we have customer data and know which customers have churned, we can train a model to predict churn for new customers by identifying patterns associated with past churn cases.

On the other hand, unsupervised learning tackles data that lacks labels or predefined outputs. The goal is to explore the data and identify hidden patterns, groupings, or structures. Without labelled examples to learn from, the model independently seeks to uncover the data's underlying patterns.

Supervised vs. Unsupervised Learning

Unsupervised learning does not aim to map inputs to outputs as supervised learning does; instead, it focuses on discovering the data's inherent structure, such as grouping similar data points through techniques like clustering.

A classic example of unsupervised learning is market segmentation, which aims to group customers into different segments based on purchasing behaviour. Unlike churn prediction, where labels indicate whether a customer has churned, market segmentation does not have predefined groups. The model must discover these segments based on similarities in the data.

Unsupervised learning is concerned with discovering and identifying regularities in the input dataset. Fortunately, in most cases, data points exhibit some form of regularity or pattern, which unsupervised learning algorithms can exploit. For instance, customers with similar purchasing behaviours may naturally form distinct groups or segments. These regularities are the foundation of unsupervised learning.

The primary objective of unsupervised learning is to gain insights from data by discovering its inherent structure without any prior labels. Techniques like clustering allow us to understand and interpret data intuitively, helping businesses make informed decisions by revealing patterns that might not be immediately obvious.

The Power of Clustering in Unsupervised Learning

One of the most popular unsupervised learning methods is clustering. Unlike supervised learning, where the goal might be to predict which customers will churn based on labelled data, clustering helps identify natural groupings of customers based on their behaviours, even when we don't know in advance which customers belong to which group.

By clustering customers based on purchasing behaviour, a company can identify distinct market segments and tailor its marketing strategies accordingly. This process allows the company to allocate resources effectively, targeting high-value customers and retaining those who might otherwise churn.

Clustering simplifies the process of understanding complex data by grouping similar data points, making it easier to comprehend the overall structure of the data. In summary, unsupervised learning is a powerful tool for discovering hidden patterns in data. By leveraging techniques like clustering, organisations can gain a deeper understanding of their data, leading to better decision-making and strategic insights. Unsupervised learning provides the foundation for advanced data exploration and analysis, whether segmenting markets, identifying trends, or detecting anomalies.

Characterising and Evaluating Clusters

Understanding how to characterise clusters and the key aspects to consider when evaluating a clustering outcome is essential in unsupervised learning. A cluster is a group of observations or data points similar to each other but dissimilar from data points in other clusters. Clustering aims to group similar items so that items within the same cluster are more alike than items in different clusters.

Unlike supervised learning, where we have a target variable or label, clustering in unsupervised learning does not have a predefined outcome. Instead, we seek to uncover natural groupings or structures in the data. Clustering methods aim to divide a dataset into relatively homogenous clusters. The objective is to maximise the distance between different clusters (inter-cluster distance) and minimise the distance within the same cluster (intra-cluster distance).

For example, imagine you have customer data from an e-commerce platform. Clustering can segment customers into groups based on their shopping behaviour. One cluster might include customers who frequently buy electronics, while another might consist of those who prefer clothing. Maximising the distance between these clusters ensures that each group is distinct, making it easier to tailor marketing strategies for each segment.

Clustering is a powerful technique that can be applied in various business scenarios, from improving marketing strategies to optimising product recommendations. By understanding the key characteristics of clustering, you can better leverage this technique to uncover valuable insights in your data.

Exploring Clustering Algorithms and Similarity Measures

Clustering algorithms work by grouping data points based on their similarities. These algorithms use various distance or similarity measures to form clusters of similar data points. To illustrate, let's consider a customer dataset that includes information on age and income. We can visualise the data using a scatter plot to understand better how customers group naturally based on these two features.

Visualising data becomes more complex when dealing with more than two features. However, in simple examples, like with only two parameters, we can easily use a scatter plot to observe potential clusters.

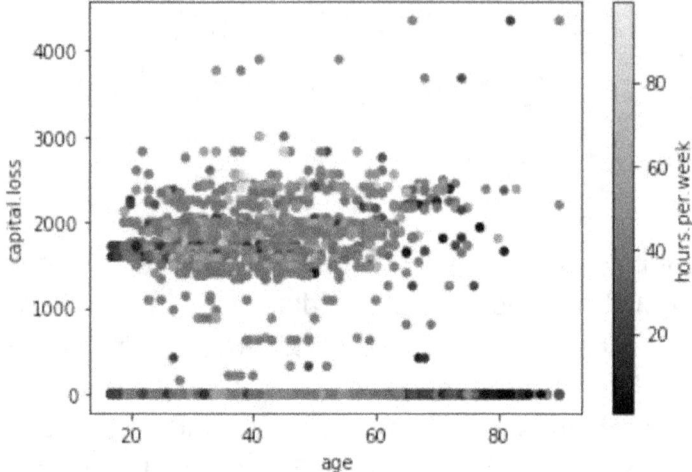

Figure 6: Example of a Scatter Plot between two parameters.

After identifying clusters visually, we can formalise the clustering process using mathematical distance measures. Two common distance measures used in clustering algorithms are Euclidean distance, which calculates the straight-line distance between two points, and Manhattan distance, which calculates the distance along axes at right angles.

Euclidean distance computes the root of the sum of the squared differences between the coordinates of two data points. It's like measuring the straight-line distance between two locations on a map. On the other hand, Manhattan distance measures the distance you would travel along a grid of city streets.

In addition to distance-based measures, there are also correlation-based distance measures. These measures consider data points similar if their features are highly correlated, even if they are physically far apart regarding Euclidean distance. Correlation-based distance measures, such as Pearson correlation distance, assess the linear relationship between features. This means two data points can be considered similar if the changes in one feature predict identical changes in another, even if the absolute values are different.

Other distance measures include Minkowski distance, which generalises Euclidean and Manhattan distances; Canberra distance, which is sensitive to differences when the data points have small values; and Chebyshev distance, which considers the maximum difference along any coordinate dimension.

Understanding how these distance measures work allows you to select the appropriate clustering algorithm for your data and gain valuable insights from the clusters formed.

Introduction to K-Means Clustering

One of the most fundamental clustering methods is K-means clustering. As discussed earlier, the goal of clustering is to group data points into clusters such that the variation between different clusters (inter-cluster distance) is maximised and the variation within each cluster (intra-cluster distance) is minimised.

Figure 7: The Farmer's Markets in the USA are divided into three clusters.

Imagine a dataset with various points scattered across a plane. The K-means algorithm works by grouping these points into clusters. The objective is to ensure that the points within each cluster are as close as possible to each other while the clusters themselves are as distinct as possible.

To visualise this, let's consider four clusters. Each cluster has a centre, known as the centroid, which is the average position of all the points within that cluster. The intra-cluster distance is calculated by measuring the distance of each point in the cluster from the centroid and averaging these distances. The goal is to make these distances as small as possible, indicating that the points are tightly packed around the centroid.

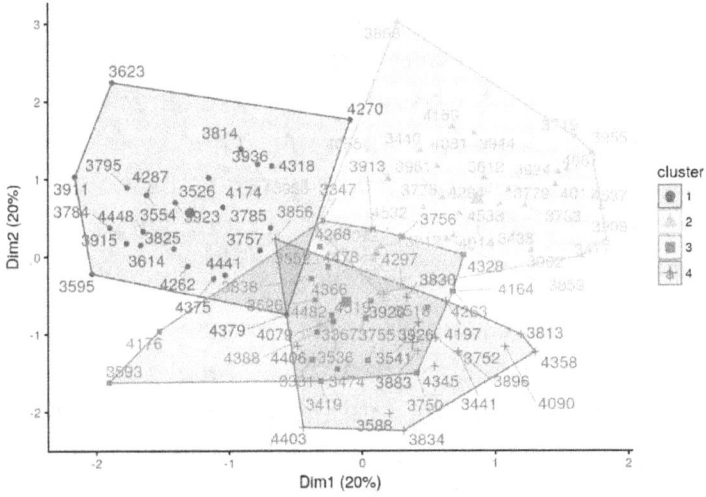

Figure 8: Example of four clusters created using the K-Means algorithm.

On the other hand, the inter-cluster distance is the distance between the centroids of different clusters. We want this distance to be as large as possible, showing that the clusters are well-separated.

The first step in the K-means algorithm is to choose the number of clusters denoted by K. This number can be based on prior knowledge or determined through experimentation. Once you've chosen K, the next step is randomly selecting K points from the data as the initial cluster centres or centroids.

With these initial centroids in place, the algorithm proceeds in iterative steps. In each iteration, every data point is assigned to the cluster with the nearest centroid. Once all the points are transferred, the centroids are recalculated as the average position of all the points within each cluster.

The algorithm repeats this process: reassigning points to the nearest centroids, recalculating the centroids, and so on until the centroids no longer move significantly, indicating that the clusters are stable. The algorithm has converged, and the data is grouped into K clusters.

K-means clustering is widely used for its simplicity and effectiveness, particularly when the number of clusters is known or can be reasonably estimated. However, it is essential to remember that the choice of K and the initial placement of centroids can significantly impact the final clusters. Techniques such as the Elbow method are often used to determine the optimal number of clusters, ensuring that the chosen K value leads to meaningful and well-separated clusters.

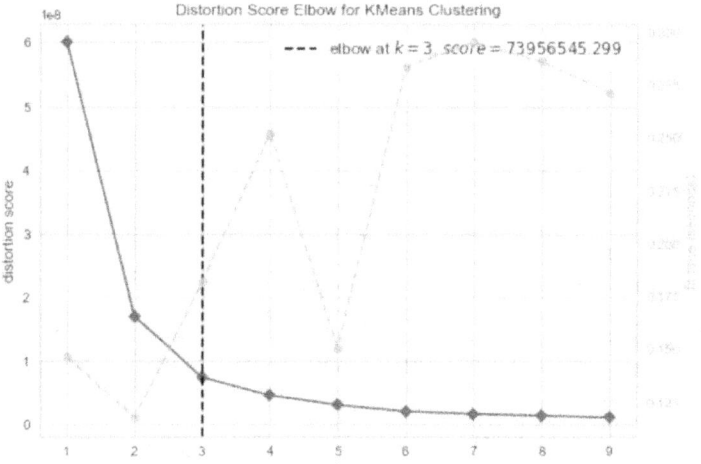

Figure 9: Determining the required number of clusters using the Elbow Method.

Hierarchical Clustering and Its Applications

In addition to K-means clustering, hierarchical clustering is another powerful method for grouping data. This technique is particularly useful when the number of clusters is unknown beforehand and when dealing with non-spherical data. Unlike K-means, hierarchical clustering does not require specifying the number of clusters in advance. Instead, it produces a set of nested clusters arranged in a tree-like structure called a dendrogram. This structure visually represents the clustering process and allows for a more nuanced interpretation of the data.

Hierarchical clustering comes in two main forms: divisive and agglomerative. Divisive hierarchical clustering starts with all data points in a single cluster and iteratively splits them into smaller clusters until each cluster contains only one sample. On the other hand, agglomerative hierarchical clustering, which is more commonly used, begins by treating each data point as its cluster. The algorithm then merges the two closest clusters at each step until all data points are combined into one cluster.

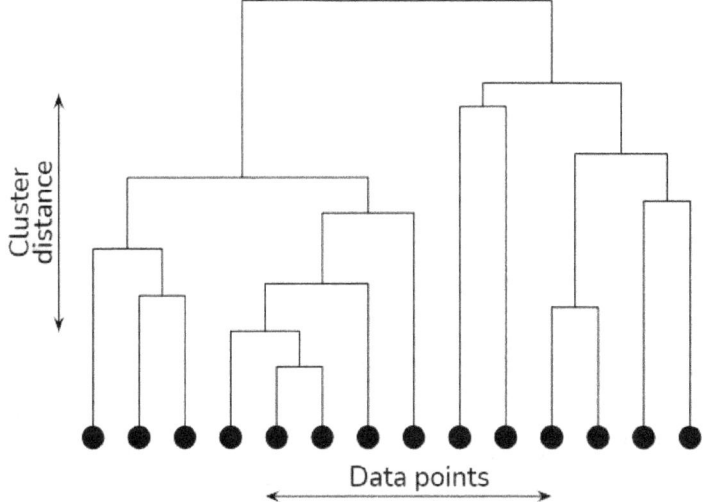

*Figure 10: A Dendrogram showing Hierarchical Clusters.
(Source: Google Images)*

The steps for performing agglomerative hierarchical clustering are as follows. First, a distance metric for all data points is computed, typically using Euclidean distance. However, other metrics can also be used depending on the data's nature. Next, each data point is treated as a separate or "singleton" cluster. The algorithm identifies and merges the two closest clusters based on a chosen linkage criterion, such as single, complete, average, or ward linkage.

Once the two closest clusters are merged, the distance metrics are updated to reflect the new cluster formation, and the process repeats. This continues until all data points are incorporated into a cluster, forming a complete dendrogram. The dendrogram allows us to decide the optimal number of clusters by visually inspecting where to "cut" the tree.

However, hierarchical clustering has its challenges. One of the main issues is its computational complexity, especially with large datasets, as merging clusters becomes increasingly resource-intensive. Additionally, hierarchical clustering is sensitive to outliers, which can distort the resulting dendrogram and the interpretation of clusters.

For example, hierarchical clustering can be used to analyse customer purchasing behaviour. By applying different linkage methods, one can observe how clusters form based on various criteria, providing insights into customer segments that might not be apparent with simpler methods like K-means.

Understanding these aspects of hierarchical clustering will help apply it more effectively, especially when dealing with complex data where traditional clustering methods may fall short.

Product Segmentation Using Hierarchical Clustering

Hierarchical clustering can also be applied effectively in product segmentation. For instance, consider a company that wants to launch a new beer brand and needs to understand the existing market segments. By analysing a dataset containing attributes like cost, calorie content, sodium content, and alcohol content of various beer brands, hierarchical clustering can reveal distinct segments within the market.

The process begins with data standardisation using a method like `StandardScaler` to ensure that all features contribute equally to the clustering process. Then, agglomerative hierarchical clustering is applied, specifying the desired number of clusters. The resulting clusters can be analysed to identify different market segments, such as lower-cost beers, health-conscious beers, and premium brands.

Hierarchical and K-means clustering can produce similar results, but hierarchical clustering offers the additional advantage of not requiring the number of clusters to be specified upfront. This flexibility is particularly useful in exploratory data analysis when the optimal number of clusters is unknown. Furthermore, the dendrogram produced by hierarchical clustering provides a visual representation of how clusters form, aiding in the interpretation of the data.

Hierarchical Clustering for Gaussian Distributed Data

Hierarchical clustering is also well-suited for Gaussian distributed data. Gaussian distribution, often called the normal distribution, is characterised by its bell-shaped curve, which is symmetric around the mean. This distribution is commonly used in statistics and data science to represent variables that cluster around a central value with a certain degree of spread.

Synthetic data can be generated using Python's `make_blobs()` function to demonstrate hierarchical clustering on Gaussian distributed data. This function allows for creating clusters of data points with specified centres and spread, following a Gaussian distribution. The generated data can be visualised using a dendrogram created with the Seaborn package's `clustermap` method or the SciPy library.

The dendrogram reveals the arrangement of clusters produced by hierarchical clustering, with vertical lines representing the merging of clusters based on their proximity. This visualisation helps identify the natural groupings within the data, providing insights into the underlying structure.

Hierarchical clustering's ability to handle Gaussian distributed data makes it valuable in various business contexts, such as customer segmentation, where understanding natural groupings can inform targeted marketing strategies or product development.

DBSCAN Clustering: A Flexible Approach for Noisy Data

DBSCAN (Density-Based Spatial Clustering of Applications with Noise) is another powerful clustering algorithm well-suited for datasets with varying densities and noise. Unlike K-means, which assumes spherical clusters and requires specifying the number of clusters beforehand, DBSCAN forms clusters based on the density of data points.

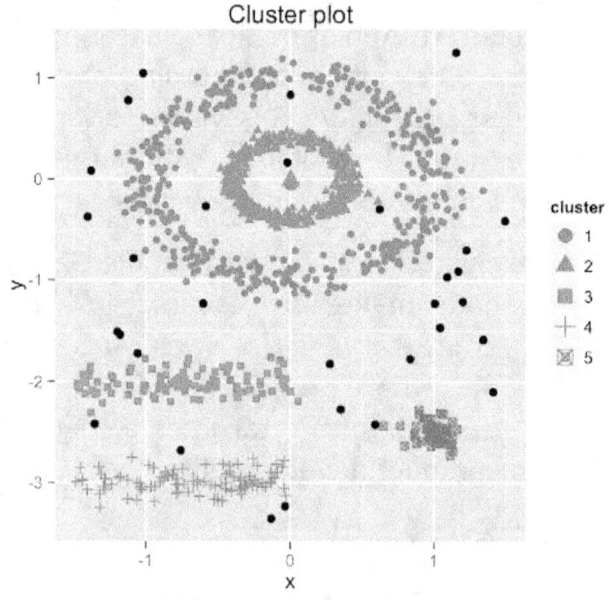

Figure 11: Example output of DBSCAN. (Source: Google Images)

DBSCAN works by assigning labels to data points based on their density. A data point is labelled as a core point if it has enough neighbouring points within a specified radius, known as `eps`. If a point has fewer neighbours than required but is within the radius of a core point, it is labelled as a border point. Any data point that does not meet these criteria is considered noise.

The clustering process in DBSCAN involves forming clusters by identifying core points or groups of core points within the `eps` distance from each other. These core points form the basis of each cluster. Border points are then assigned to the clusters formed by the core points, effectively grouping them based on proximity.

One key advantage of DBSCAN is that it does not require specifying the number of clusters in advance, making it highly effective at discovering clusters of varying shapes and sizes. Additionally, DBSCAN excels at identifying and removing noise from the dataset, an area where other clustering methods, like K-means, often struggle.

To implement DBSCAN in practice, the Scikit-learn library in Python can be used. When using DBSCAN, two critical parameters must be specified: `eps` and `min_samples`. The `eps` parameter defines the maximum distance between two points for them to be considered in the same neighbourhood, while `min_samples` sets the minimum number of points required to form a dense region or cluster. Adjusting these parameters based on the dataset's characteristics is essential to achieving meaningful clustering results.

A practical example of DBSCAN's application could be in geographical data analysis, where the goal is to identify densely populated areas while excluding sparsely populated regions. In this context, DBSCAN effectively identifies clusters without needing to predefine the number of clusters, and it automatically handles outliers by treating them as noise.

Conclusion

In the field of data science, both supervised and unsupervised learning methods play crucial roles in extracting valuable insights from data. While supervised learning focuses on predicting outcomes based on labelled data, unsupervised learning is geared towards exploring data to identify hidden patterns and structures. Clustering, a key technique in unsupervised learning, allows businesses to discover natural groupings within their data, enabling more informed decision-making.

This article comprehensively overviews various clustering techniques, including K-means, hierarchical clustering, and DBSCAN. Each method has strengths and limitations, making it suitable for different data types and analytical goals. By understanding these techniques and how to apply them effectively, data scientists and business analysts can uncover valuable insights that drive strategic decisions and improve organisational outcomes.

References

- Bishop, C. M. (2006). Pattern Recognition and Machine Learning. Springer. ISBN: 978-0387310732
- Ester, M., Kriegel, H.-P., Sander, J., & Xu, X. (1996). A Density-Based Algorithm for Discovering Clusters in Large Spatial Databases with Noise. Proceedings of the Second International Conference on Knowledge Discovery and Data Mining, 226-231. ISBN: 1-57735-004-9
- James, G., Witten, D., Hastie, T., & Tibshirani, R. (2013). An Introduction to Statistical Learning: with Applications in R. Springer. ISBN: 978-1461471370
- Pedregosa, F., Varoquaux, G., Gramfort, A., Michel, V., Thirion, B., Grisel, O., ... & Duchesnay, E. (2011). Scikit-learn: Machine Learning in Python. Journal of Machine Learning Research, 12, 2825-2830. Available at:

https://jmlr.csail.mit.edu/papers/volume12/pedregosa11a/pedregosa11a.pdf
- Tan, P.-N., Steinbach, M., & Kumar, V. (2006). Introduction to Data Mining. Pearson Education. ISBN: 978-0321321367

Additional Reading Material

- Bishop, C. M. (2006). Pattern Recognition and Machine Learning. Springer. ISBN: 978-0387310732
- Hastie, T., Tibshirani, R., & Friedman, J. (2009). The Elements of Statistical Learning: Data Mining, Inference, and Prediction. Springer. ISBN: 978-0387848570
- James, G., Witten, D., Hastie, T., & Tibshirani, R. (2013). An Introduction to Statistical Learning: with Applications in R. Springer. ISBN: 978-1461471370
- Scikit-learn Documentation. Available at: https://scikit-learn.org/stable/documentation.html
- Witten, I. H., & Frank, E. (2016). Data Mining: Practical Machine Learning Tools

and Techniques. Morgan Kaufmann. ISBN: 978-0128042915

Exploring the Fundamentals of Artificial Neural Networks and Their Applications

Abstract

Artificial neural networks (ANNs) are a foundational class of machine learning algorithms inspired by the structure and function of the human brain. This article delves into the basics of ANNs, covering their architecture, including perceptrons, multilayer perceptrons, and advanced forms like convolutional and recurrent neural networks. It also explores the critical role of backpropagation in training ANNs, highlights their applications across various industries, and discusses their benefits and limitations. Additionally, the article introduces deep learning concepts, examines popular deep learning libraries, and explains the significance of hyperparameters in neural network performance.

Lastly, the article introduces Long Short-Term Memory (LSTM) networks and Generative Pre-Trained Transformers (GPTs). These two advanced architectures address specific challenges in sequential data processing and natural language generation.

Introduction

Artificial neural networks (ANNs) have become one of the most significant breakthroughs in machine learning, emulating the brain's ability to recognise patterns and make decisions. These networks consist of interconnected processing nodes called neurons, which receive inputs, perform mathematical operations, and generate outputs. While the earliest form of neural networks, the perceptron, was limited in its ability to solve complex problems, modern neural networks have evolved to include sophisticated architectures like convolutional neural networks (CNNs) and recurrent neural networks (RNNs), enabling them to excel in specialised tasks such as image recognition and sequence prediction.

The Basics of Artificial Neural Networks

The perceptron, a basic mathematical model of a biological neuron, is the foundation of neural networks. Each neuron receives one or more inputs weighted according to their importance, which is then summed and passed through a non-linear activation function to produce the neuron's output. This non-linearity is crucial as it enables the network to model complex relationships between inputs and outputs.

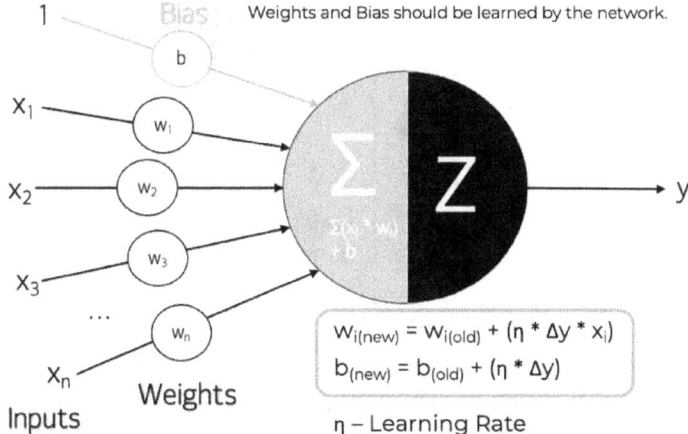

Figure 12: Schematic diagram of an Artificial Neuron (a Perceptron). Σ is the Summation function, and Z is the Activation Function.

Modern neural networks typically consist of multiple layers of neurons, allowing them to learn hierarchical representations of data. These layers include the input layer, hidden layers, and output layer. The hidden layers perform the bulk of the computation, with different activation functions like ReLU, sigmoid, and softmax being used based on the task's requirements.

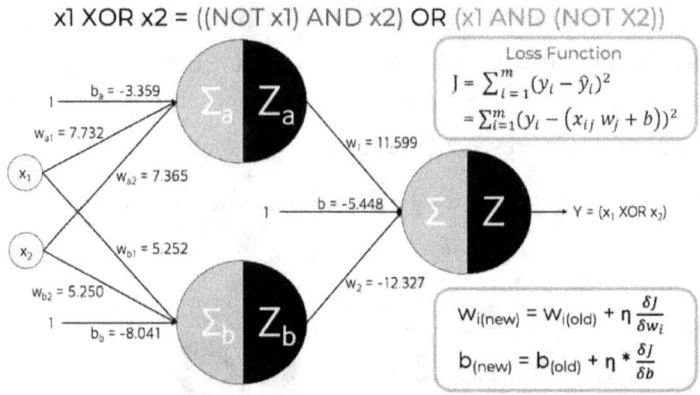

Figure 13: A Multi-Layer Perceptron (MLP) to solve the XOR problem.

Early neural networks faced significant challenges in modelling non-linear relationships, notably their inability to solve the XOR problem. This limitation highlighted the need for more complex architectures, leading to the development of multilayer perceptrons (MLPs) that can learn non-linear functions by organising neurons into multiple interconnected layers.

Backpropagation: The Key to Learning in Neural Networks

Backpropagation is a crucial algorithm that enables neural networks to learn from data. As a supervised learning method, backpropagation adjusts the network's weights to minimise errors between predicted and actual outputs. This process involves calculating the gradient of the loss function concerning each weight using the chain rule, which guides the adjustment of weights in the opposite direction of the gradient.

The effectiveness of backpropagation relies on different activation functions, such as ReLU or sigmoid, which allow the gradient to be computed efficiently. During training, the network iteratively updates its weights through multiple forward and backward passes, gradually reducing the overall error.

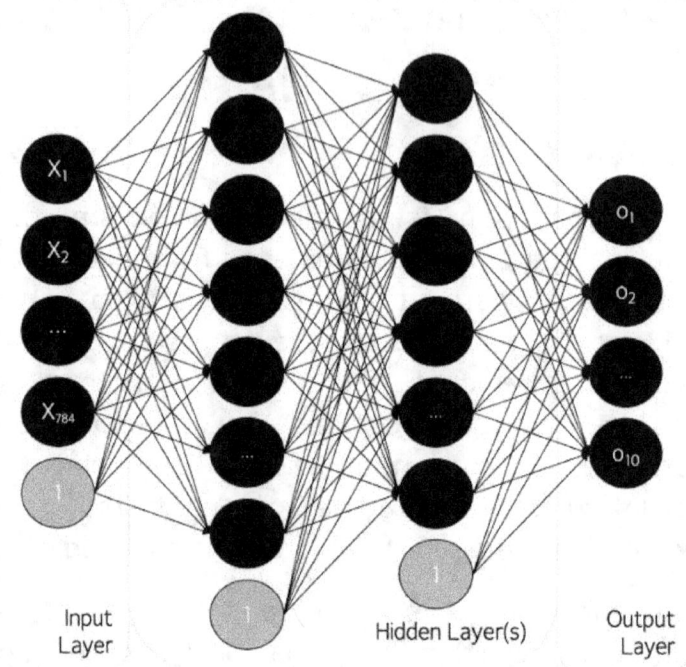

Figure 14: A Deep Neural Network for detecting handwritten digits using the MNIST dataset.

Applications, Benefits, and Limitations of Neural Networks

Neural networks have gained prominence since 2012, particularly with the advent of deep learning and GPUs to accelerate backpropagation. This development made training large and complex models feasible, leading to breakthroughs in image classification, natural language processing (NLP), and gameplaying. For instance, AlexNet's success in image classification in 2012 and AlphaGo's victory over the World Champion in Go, Lee Sedol, in 2016 are notable milestones.

Neural networks are particularly well-suited for problems involving large amounts of data and complex patterns. They are widely used in predictive analytics, fraud detection, sentiment analysis, recommender systems, and image and speech recognition. These applications span various industries, including finance, healthcare, and e-commerce, providing valuable insights and predictive capabilities that drive business growth.

Despite their advantages, neural networks have limitations. Training deep neural networks often requires large amounts of high-quality data, significant computational resources, and time. Moreover, the "black box" nature of neural networks makes interpreting how they arrive at certain decisions challenging, hindering stakeholder trust and acceptance. Additionally, the skills gap in neural network development and deployment remains a barrier to widespread adoption.

Deep Learning: Expanding the Capabilities of Neural Networks

Deep learning, a subset of machine learning, leverages artificial neural networks with multiple layers to extract higher-level features from raw input data. Unlike traditional machine learning algorithms, deep learning models can automatically discover relevant features, making them particularly effective for tasks like image recognition and NLP.

Deep learning's power lies in its ability to learn hierarchical representations, with each layer building on the previous one to detect increasingly complex patterns. Popular deep-learning architectures include CNNs for image data, RNNs for sequential data, LSTMs for long-term dependencies, and transformers for NLP tasks. These models have revolutionised advertising, healthcare, and security, enabling significant advancements in disease diagnosis, automated content generation, and personalised recommendations.

Neural Network Libraries: Tools for Building and Training Models

Several libraries have been developed to facilitate the building and training of deep learning models. TensorFlow, developed by Google, is one of the most popular deep learning libraries, offering GPU acceleration to speed up training. Keras, now integrated with TensorFlow, provides a high-level API for rapid experimentation, making it easier for users to build and train models without delving into the complexities of lower-level libraries.

PyTorch, developed by Facebook, has gained popularity due to its ease of use and dynamic computation graph, which allows for more flexibility in model building. These libraries represent data using tensors and multi-dimensional arrays like NumPy arrays. Tensors are the fundamental building blocks of deep learning models, enabling efficient computation on GPUs.

Choosing Neural Network Parameters and Hyperparameters

The performance of neural networks heavily depends on the choice of parameters and hyperparameters. Parameters are the model's coefficients, optimised during training to minimise error. Hyperparameters, however, are set manually before training begins and govern the training process itself, such as the number of hidden layers, learning rate, and batch size.

Selecting the appropriate hyperparameters often requires experimentation and cross-validation. For instance, choosing the number of hidden layers and neurons per layer can significantly impact the model's ability to learn and generalise. Similarly, setting the learning rate and batch size affects training speed and convergence stability.

Regularisation techniques, such as L1 and L2 regularisation and dropout, prevent overfitting by adding penalties for large weights or randomly dropping out neurons during training. Optimisers like Adam and SGD are crucial in updating the network's weights to minimise the loss function.

Advanced Architectures: LSTMs, GRUs, and GPTs

Long-short-term memory (LSTM) and Gated Recurrent Unit (GRU) networks are a type of RNN designed to address the vanishing gradient problem in traditional RNNs, enabling them to learn long-term dependencies. Among other applications, LSTMs and GRUs are widely used in time series prediction, machine translation, and speech recognition.

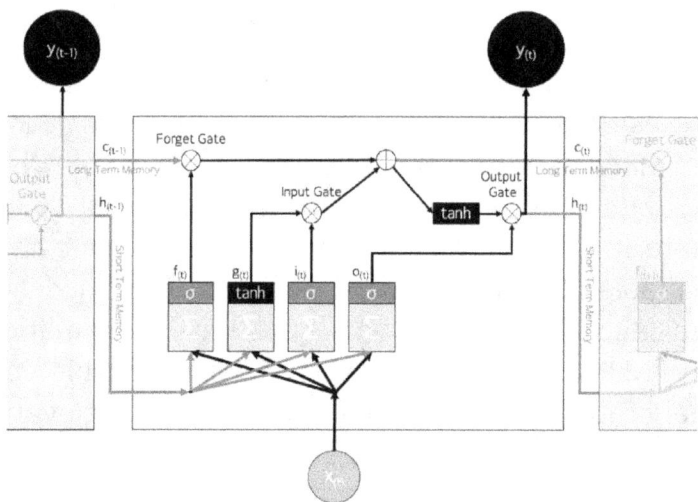

Figure 15: LSTM Architecture.

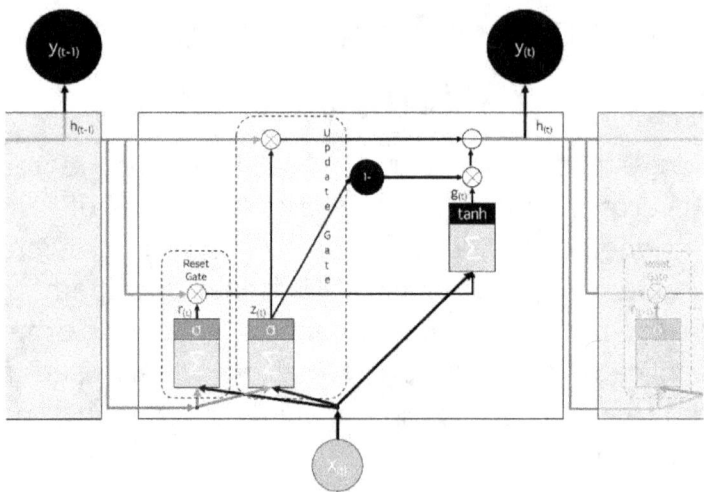

Figure 16: GRU Architecture.

Transformers, including Generative Pre-Trained Transformers (GPTs), represent a significant advancement in deep learning. Unlike RNNs, LSTMs, and GRUs, transformers process input data in parallel, making them more efficient and capable of handling larger datasets. GPT models, developed by OpenAI, have set new benchmarks in NLP, with GPT-3 and GPT-4 capable of generating coherent and contextually relevant text over long sequences.

ChatGPT, based on GPT architecture, exemplifies the power of transformers in generating human-like conversational responses. However, while transformers excel in generating text, they do not replace search engines like Google, which rely on complex algorithms to index and rank vast amounts of information.

Conclusion

Artificial neural networks, from basic perceptrons to advanced architectures like LSTMs and transformers, have transformed machine learning and AI, enabling significant advancements across various industries. While they offer powerful tools for pattern recognition, predictive analytics, and decision-making, neural networks also present challenges regarding training requirements, interpretability, and deployment. As deep learning continues to evolve, with models like GPT and BERT pushing the boundaries of what's possible, neural networks' role in shaping AI's future is more crucial than ever.

References

- Hochreiter, S., & Schmidhuber, J. (1997). Long short-term memory. Neural Computation, 9(8), 1735-1780. DOI:

https://doi.org/10.1162/neco.1997.9.8.1735
- Krizhevsky, A., Sutskever, I., & Hinton, G. E. (2012). ImageNet classification with deep convolutional neural networks. Advances in Neural Information Processing Systems, 25, 1097-1105. DOI: https://doi.org/10.1145/3065386
- LeCun, Y., Bengio, Y., & Hinton, G. (2015). Deep learning. Nature, 521(7553), 436-444. DOI: https://doi.org/10.1038/nature14539
- Rumelhart, D. E., Hinton, G. E., & Williams, R. J. (1986). Learning representations by back-propagating errors. Nature, 323(6088), 533-536. DOI: https://doi.org/10.1038/323533a0
- Vaswani, A., Shazeer, N., Parmar, N., Uszkoreit, J., Jones, L., Gomez, A. N., ... & Polosukhin, I. (2017). Attention is all you need. Advances in Neural Information Processing Systems, 30, 5998-6008. DOI: https://doi.org/10.48550/arXiv.1706.03762

Additional Reading Material

- Aggarwal, C. C. (2018). Neural Networks and Deep Learning: A Textbook. Springer. ISBN: 978-3319944630
- Brown, T. B., Mann, B., Ryder, N., Subbiah, M., Kaplan, J., Dhariwal, P., ... & Amodei, D. (2020). Language Models are Few-Shot Learners. Advances in Neural Information Processing Systems, 33, 1877-1901. DOI: https://doi.org/10.48550/arXiv.2005.14165
- Chollet, F. (2018). Deep Learning with Python. Manning Publications. ISBN: 978-1617294433
- Géron, A. (2019). Hands-On Machine Learning with Scikit-Learn, Keras, and TensorFlow (2nd ed.). O'Reilly Media. ISBN: 978-1492032649
- Goodfellow, I., Bengio, Y., & Courville, A. (2016). Deep Learning. MIT Press. ISBN: 978-0262035613
- Silver, D., Huang, A., Maddison, C. J., Guez, A., Sifre, L., Van Den Driessche, G., ... & Hassabis, D. (2016). Mastering the game of Go with deep neural networks and tree

search. Nature, 529(7587), 484-489. DOI: https://doi.org/10.1038/nature16961
- Vaswani, A., Shazeer, N., Parmar, N., Uszkoreit, J., Jones, L., Gomez, A. N., ... & Polosukhin, I. (2017). Attention is All You Need. Advances in Neural Information Processing Systems, 30, 5998-6008. DOI: https://doi.org/10.48550/arXiv.1706.03762

Reinforcement Learning

Abstract

Reinforcement learning (RL), a critical branch of machine learning, has emerged as a powerful tool for solving complex problems across various sectors, including healthcare, robotics, gaming, and marketing. Unlike supervised and unsupervised learning, RL is inspired by the human way of learning through trial and error, making decisions based on the consequences of actions. This article delves into the fundamental concepts of reinforcement learning, explores its applications, and examines the tools and techniques that drive its success. We also discuss the inherent challenges, such as the exploration-exploitation dilemma and the difficulties of real-world deployment. Through examples and case studies, we demonstrate how RL revolutionises industries by enabling systems to learn from their environments and optimise decision-making processes.

Introduction

Reinforcement learning (RL) is one of the three primary types of machine learning, alongside supervised and unsupervised learning. RL is unique because it is based on how humans learn through experience. It involves an agent interacting with an environment, making decisions, and receiving feedback through rewards or punishments. Over time, the agent knows to optimise its actions to maximise cumulative rewards. This trial-and-error approach allows RL models to adapt to new situations and make decisions without requiring a pre-labelled dataset, making RL particularly suited for dynamic and uncertain environments.

Supervised and Unsupervised Learning: A Brief Comparison

In supervised learning, algorithms are trained on labelled data, where each input's desired output is known. This method is powerful when the data is accurately labelled and can produce highly reliable models for tasks such as classification and regression.

On the other hand, unsupervised learning deals with data containing only inputs with no predefined labels. The algorithm must identify hidden structures or patterns within the data, making it versatile for exploratory data analysis. Techniques like clustering and association rule learning are commonly used in unsupervised learning to uncover meaningful groupings or relationships within the data.

While both supervised and unsupervised learning have their strengths, they rely heavily on the quality and structure of the input data. RL differs fundamentally by not requiring labelled data or predefined outputs. Instead, it learns from the consequences of actions within an environment, making it more akin to human learning.

Reinforcement Learning: How It Works

In reinforcement learning, the agent operates within an environment and takes actions based on its current state. The environment then responds to these actions, transitioning to a new state and providing feedback through rewards or penalties. The agent aims to maximise the cumulative reward over time by learning the optimal policy—a strategy that dictates the best action in each state.

A classic example of RL is training an autonomous vehicle. The agent (vehicle) must learn to navigate through various environments (roads, traffic, weather conditions) by making decisions (steering, braking, accelerating) and receiving feedback based on the outcomes (avoiding collisions, maintaining speed, following traffic rules). Over time, the vehicle learns the optimal driving strategy by balancing the trade-off between exploration (trying new routes or manoeuvres) and exploitation (relying on a known successful strategy).

Markov Decision Processes (MDP)

At the heart of reinforcement learning is the Markov Decision Process (MDP), a mathematical framework used to model decision-making in environments where outcomes are partly random and partly under the control of a decision-maker. The MDP framework is crucial because it provides a structured way to describe the problem the RL agent is trying to solve.

Four key components define an MDP are as follows.

1. **States (S)**: These represent all situations where the agent could find itself.
2. **Actions (A)**: The agent can make these possible decisions or moves.
3. **Transition Function (T)**: This gives the probability of moving from one state to another after taking a specific action.
4. **Reward Function (R)**: This provides the immediate reward received after transitioning from one state to another due to an action.

The agent's goal is to select actions that maximise the expected cumulative reward over time, referred to as the long-term measure of total reward.

Q-Learning

Q-learning is a fundamental reinforcement learning algorithm that builds on the MDP framework but is "model-free," meaning it does not require knowledge of the MDP's transition and reward functions. Instead, Q-learning learns directly from interactions with the environment.

In Q-learning, the agent maintains a table of Q-values, where each entry represents the expected cumulative reward (or "quality") of taking a certain action in a given state and following the optimal policy after that. The agent updates these Q-values iteratively based on the rewards it receives from the environment.

The Q-learning update rule is as follows.

$$Q(s, a) \leftarrow Q(s, a) + \alpha [r + \gamma \max_{\acute{a}} Q(\acute{s}, \acute{a}) - Q(s, a)]$$

where:

- $Q(s, a)$ is the Q-value for state s and action a.
- α is the learning rate.
- r is the reward received after taking action a in state s.
- γ is the discount factor determining future rewards' importance.

- $\acute{s}$ is the new state after taking action a.
- $\max_{\acute{a}} Q(\acute{s}, \acute{a})$ is the maximum Q-value for the new state $\acute{s}$.

Over time, Q-learning converges to the optimal policy, allowing the agent to make decisions that maximise the cumulative reward.

Applications of Q-Learning

Q-learning has been applied in various domains, from robotics to finance. For instance, in robotics, Q-learning can help a robot navigate a maze by learning the optimal path to a goal while avoiding obstacles. In finance, Q-learning can be used to develop trading strategies by learning to buy, sell, or hold assets based on market conditions to maximise profit.

One of the most famous Q-learning applications is in the AlphaGo development by DeepMind. AlphaGo used reinforcement learning, including Q-learning techniques, to master the game of Go, eventually defeating world champion Lee Sedol in 2016. This groundbreaking achievement in AI demonstrated the power of reinforcement learning to tackle complex, dynamic environments.

Tools for Reinforcement Learning

Several tools and libraries have been developed to facilitate the implementation of reinforcement learning algorithms. Among the most widely used are TensorFlow, Keras, PyTorch, OpenAI Gym, and RLlib.

TensorFlow, developed by Google, is a popular machine-learning library that supports reinforcement learning. It provides a comprehensive ecosystem for building and training models, with TensorFlow Agents offering a specialised library for designing and testing RL algorithms. TensorLayer, an extension of TensorFlow, provides additional modules tailored for real-world RL applications.

Keras, a high-level API running on top of TensorFlow, simplifies the process of building neural networks and is particularly useful for fast experimentation in RL. Its ease of use and integration with TensorFlow make it a popular choice for researchers and developers.

PyTorch, an open-source deep learning library developed by Facebook, is another favourite among RL practitioners. PyTorch is known for its dynamic computation graph and strong GPU acceleration, which allows for more flexible and efficient model development, particularly in policy-based reinforcement learning.

OpenAI Gym is a toolkit that provides various environments for testing and developing RL algorithms. It is compatible with both TensorFlow and PyTorch, making it an essential resource for anyone working in the field of RL. OpenAI Gym includes environments for classic problems like CartPole and Mountain Car and complex simulations for games like Atari.

RLlib, built on top of Ray, is an open-source library designed for scalable and distributed RL workloads. It supports production-level RL applications across various industries, from climate control and industrial automation to finance and robotics. RLlib's flexibility and scalability make it a powerful tool for deploying RL models in real-world settings.

Challenges in Reinforcement Learning

Despite its potential, reinforcement learning faces several challenges. One of the most significant is the exploration-exploitation trade-off. The agent must balance exploring new actions to discover their potential rewards with exploiting known actions that have previously yielded high rewards. Striking this balance is crucial for efficient learning and long-term success.

Another challenge is preparing realistic simulation environments. While creating environments for games like chess or Go is relatively straightforward, simulating the complexities of real-world tasks, such as autonomous driving, requires sophisticated tools and considerable computational resources. Transferring models from simulated environments to real-world applications is another hurdle, as the real world is often more unpredictable and less forgiving than a controlled simulation.

Catastrophic forgetting is another issue, where an RL agent may "forget" previously learned tasks when acquiring new knowledge. This challenge is particularly relevant in continual learning scenarios, where the agent must adapt to new tasks without losing proficiency in previously learned ones.

Applications of Reinforcement Learning

Reinforcement learning has revolutionised various industries by enabling systems to learn from interaction with their environments and make decisions that adapt to changing conditions.

In healthcare, RL optimises treatment plans, suggests appropriate drug dosages, and enhances surgical procedures through advanced systems like the Da Vinci robot. RL-trained robots navigate complex environments in robotics, performing highly autonomous tasks like quality testing and packaging.

The gaming industry has seen significant advancements with RL, where AI agents can learn complex strategies and adapt to players' behaviours. AlphaGo, developed by DeepMind, is a prime example of RL's power, as it defeated world champion Go players through self-play and reinforcement learning.

In the automotive industry, RL is critical in developing self-driving cars. RL models are trained to optimise routes, make real-time decisions, and adapt to dynamic driving conditions, making autonomous vehicles safer and more efficient.

Natural language processing (NLP) also benefits from RL, with applications in text summarisation, dialogue generation, and machine translation. RL models improve over time by learning from user interactions, resulting in more relevant and accurate outputs.

RL optimises cooling systems in data centres, reducing energy consumption and improving efficiency. Adaptive traffic signal control is another promising application in which RL models adjust traffic lights based on real-time conditions to reduce congestion and improve traffic flow.

In marketing, RL models predict customer behaviour, personalise content, and optimise digital campaigns, increasing engagement and profit margins. Supply chain management also benefits from RL, with models optimising inventory planning, bin packing, and machine calibration.

Conclusion

Reinforcement learning is a powerful tool that has transformed numerous industries by enabling systems to learn from experience and make decisions that adapt to changing environments. Its ability to solve complex problems that were previously intractable has made RL an invaluable asset in the modern AI landscape. However, RL also presents challenges, including computational demands, the exploration-exploitation trade-off, and the difficulties of real-world deployment. By understanding and addressing these challenges, we can continue to harness the potential of reinforcement learning to drive innovation and improve decision-making across various domains.

References

- Brockman, G., Cheung, V., Pettersson, L., Schneider, J., Schulman, J., Tang, J., & Zaremba, W. (2016). OpenAI Gym. arXiv preprint arXiv:1606.01540. DOI: https://doi.org/10.48550/arXiv.1606.01540
- Lillicrap, T. P., Hunt, J. J., Pritzel, A., Heess, N., Erez, T., Tassa, Y., ... & Wierstra, D.

(2016). Continuous control with deep reinforcement learning. arXiv preprint arXiv:1509.02971. DOI: https://doi.org/10.48550/arXiv.1509.02971
- Mnih, V., Kavukcuoglu, K., Silver, D., Rusu, A. A., Veness, J., Bellemare, M. G., ... & Hassabis, D. (2015). Human-level control through deep reinforcement learning. Nature, 518(7540), 529-533. DOI: https://doi.org/10.1038/nature14236
- Sutton, R. S., & Barto, A. G. (2018). Reinforcement Learning: An Introduction (2nd ed.). MIT Press. ISBN: 9780262039246

Additional Reading Material

- Francois-Lavet, V., Henderson, P., Islam, R., Bellemare, M. G., & Pineau, J. (2018). An introduction to deep reinforcement learning. Foundations and Trends in Machine Learning, 11(3-4), 219-354. DOI: https://doi.org/10.1561/2200000071

- Li, Y. (2017). Deep reinforcement learning: An overview. arXiv preprint arXiv:1701.07274. DOI: https://doi,org/10.48550/arXiv.1701.07274
- Puterman, M. L. (2014). Markov Decision Processes: Discrete Stochastic Dynamic Programming. John Wiley & Sons. ISBN: 9781118625873
- Silver, D., Huang, A., Maddison, C. J., Guez, A., Sifre, L., Van Den Driessche, G., ... & Hassabis, D. (2016). Mastering the game of Go with deep neural networks and tree search. Nature, 529(7587), 484-489. DOI: https://doi,org/10.1038/nature16961

Demystifying Time Series Forecasting and Decomposition

Abstract

Time series forecasting and decomposition are essential tools in data analysis, enabling organisations to predict future trends based on historical data. This article explores the fundamental concepts of time series, including its components—trend, seasonality, cycles, and irregularities—and how decomposition can enhance forecasting accuracy. We delve into forecasting methods, such as moving averages, ARIMA, and machine learning models, and discuss their applications in real-world scenarios. By understanding and applying these techniques, decision-makers can anticipate trends, mitigate risks, and capitalise on opportunities in dynamic business environments.

Introduction

In today's data-driven world, understanding and predicting trends from historical data is critical for making informed decisions. Time series forecasting offers a powerful method for predicting future values based on past observations, making it indispensable in finance, marketing, and operations management. Whether you're forecasting sales figures, stock prices, or website traffic, mastering time series analysis allows you to navigate uncertainties and strategically plan.

A time series is a sequence of data points recorded at successive intervals, providing a chronological perspective on how a particular variable changes over time. This sequential nature makes time series data uniquely suited for identifying patterns that can guide future predictions. By dissecting the components of time series data—trend, seasonality, cycles, and irregularities—analysts can gain deeper insights into the factors driving changes, ultimately leading to more accurate and actionable forecasts.

Understanding Time Series Components

Time series data is more than just a collection of numbers over time; it encapsulates complex patterns that reflect underlying processes and behaviours. The key components of time series data are as follows.

Trend: This component represents the long-term direction in which the data moves, whether upward, downward, or stable. For example, a steadily increasing trend in sales data may indicate overall business growth.

Seasonality: Seasonality captures periodic fluctuations that recur regularly, such as monthly, quarterly, or annually. External factors like holidays, weather, or economic cycles often drive these patterns. For instance, a retail store might experience higher sales during the holiday season each year.

Cycles: Unlike seasonality, cycles refer to long-term fluctuations not tied to a fixed calendar period. Broader economic conditions, industry-specific factors, or technological advancements can influence these. For example, the business cycle includes phases of expansion and contraction that affect demand over several years.

Irregularities (Noise): These are unpredictable variations in the data caused by random events, such as natural disasters, political instability, or sudden market changes. While these fluctuations can obscure underlying patterns, they are crucial for understanding the complete picture.

The Importance of Decomposition in Time Series Analysis

Decomposition breaks down time series data into its constituent components—trend, seasonality, cycles, and noise. By isolating these elements, analysts can better understand the factors influencing the data, leading to more accurate predictions.

For instance, separating the seasonal component from the trend allows businesses to forecast demand more accurately during peak periods without being misled by short-term fluctuations. Similarly, identifying and adjusting for cyclic patterns helps organisations prepare for economic downturns or capitalise on periods of growth.

Forecasting Methods in Time Series Analysis

Forecasting time series data involves using historical patterns to predict future values. Various methods can be employed depending on the data's complexity and the accuracy required.

Moving Averages

The moving average is a fundamental technique that shortens short-term fluctuations to highlight long-term trends. This method filters out noise by calculating the average of a subset of data points and "moving" through the series, making it easier to identify underlying patterns. For example, a 12-month moving average can reveal whether sales are consistently rising, falling, or stable.

Advantages
- Simple to understand and implement.
- Effective at smoothing out noise and revealing trends.

Limitations
- It may not capture sudden shifts in the data.
- It could be better for data with strong seasonality or cyclical patterns.

Exponential Smoothing

Exponential smoothing assigns exponentially decreasing weights to past observations, giving more importance to recent data points. This method is particularly effective for data with trends or seasonality, as it adapts to changes more quickly than simple moving averages.

Types of Exponential Smoothing
- **Single Exponential Smoothing**: Suitable for data without a trend or seasonality.
- **Double Exponential Smoothing**: Accounts for trends in the data.

- **Triple Exponential Smoothing (Holt-Winters Method)**: Incorporates trend and seasonality, making it ideal for forecasting data with regular seasonal fluctuations.

Advantages

- Flexibility in handling different types of data.
- Requires minimal computational power.

Limitations

- May need to perform better with highly volatile or complex data.

Autoregressive (AR) Model

The autoregressive model predicts future values using a linear combination of past values. It assumes that the current value of the series depends on its previous values, making it particularly useful for data with strong temporal dependencies, such as stock prices or sales figures.

Advantages
- Captures temporal dependencies effectively.
- Relatively easy to implement.

Limitations
- Requires stationary data (constant mean and variance over time).
- It may only handle seasonality or cyclic patterns well with modifications.

ARMA and ARIMA Models

The ARMA (Autoregressive Moving Average) model combines the AR model's autoregression with a moving average component to capture both past values and errors in the data. The ARIMA (Autoregressive Integrated Moving Average) model extends ARMA to handle non-stationary data by introducing differencing to stabilise the mean.

Applications
- Forecasting stock prices, sales trends, and other financial metrics.

- Modelling time series data in economics and engineering.

Advantages
- Provides a robust framework for handling a wide range of time series data.
- It can be extended to handle seasonality (SARIMA) and other complexities.

Limitations
- Requires careful tuning of parameters.
- It can be computationally intensive for large datasets.

Machine Learning Models (e.g., LSTM, Gradient Boosting)

Machine learning models, such as Long Short-Term Memory (LSTM) networks and Gradient Boosting Machines (GBM), offer advanced capabilities for handling complex, non-linear relationships in time series data. LSTM networks are particularly well-suited for sequential data, capturing long-term dependencies and temporal patterns that traditional models may miss.

Advantages
- Can model complex, non-linear patterns.
- Adaptable to various types of data.

Limitations
- Requires significant computational resources.
- It may require more data and fine-tuning compared to traditional methods.

Applications of Time Series Forecasting

Time series forecasting is widely used across industries to inform strategic decisions.

- **Retail**: Predicting product demand during peak seasons helps optimise inventory levels and reduce stockouts or overstocking.

- **Finance**: Forecasting stock prices and economic indicators guides investment decisions and risk management.
- **Healthcare**: Predicting patient admissions or disease outbreaks aids resource allocation and planning.
- **Energy**: Forecasting energy demand ensures efficient distribution and reduces waste.

Conclusion

Time series forecasting and decomposition are powerful tools for turning historical data into actionable insights. By understanding the components of a time series and applying the appropriate forecasting methods, organisations can anticipate trends, mitigate risks, and seize opportunities in a competitive landscape. Whether using simple moving averages or advanced machine learning models, mastering these techniques empowers decision-makers to make data-driven decisions that drive success and sustainability.

References

- Box, G. E. P., Jenkins, G. M., & Reinsel, G. C. (2015). Time Series Analysis: Forecasting and Control (5th ed.). Wiley. ISBN: 978-1118675021
- Chatfield, C. (2003). The Analysis of Time Series: An Introduction (6th ed.). CRC Press. ISBN: 978-1584883173
- Hamilton, J. D. (1994). Time Series Analysis. Princeton University Press. ISBN: 978-0691042893
- Holt, C. C. (2004). Forecasting seasonals and trends by exponentially weighted moving averages. International Journal of Forecasting, 20(1), 5-10. DOI: https://doi.org/10.1016/j.ijforecast.2003.09.015
- Hyndman, R. J., & Athanasopoulos, G. (2018). Forecasting: Principles and Practice (2nd ed.). OTexts. ISBN: 978-0987507112

Additional Reading Material

- Diebold, F. X. (2012). Elements of Forecasting (4th ed.). Cengage Learning. ISBN: 978-0324359047
- Hastie, T., Tibshirani, R., & Friedman, J. (2009). The Elements of Statistical Learning: Data Mining, Inference, and Prediction (2nd ed.). Springer. ISBN: 978-0387848570
- Makridakis, S., Wheelwright, S. C., & Hyndman, R. J. (1998). Forecasting: Methods and Applications (3rd ed.). Wiley. ISBN: 978-0471532330
- Shumway, R. H., & Stoffer, D. S. (2017). Time Series Analysis and Its Applications: With R Examples (4th ed.). Springer. ISBN: 978-3319524511
- Tsay, R. S. (2010). Analysis of Financial Time Series (3rd ed.). Wiley. ISBN: 978-0470414354

Navigating the Complex World of Natural Language Processing

Abstract

Natural Language Processing (NLP) is a critical field of artificial intelligence that focuses on enabling machines to understand, interpret, and generate human language. This article explores the fundamental concepts of NLP, including Natural Language Understanding (NLU) and Natural Language Generation (NLG), and their applications in various domains, such as search engines, conversational interfaces, document processing, and machine translation. It also delves into the intricacies of NLP tasks, such as text classification, sentiment analysis, and named entity recognition. It discusses the challenges posed by linguistic ambiguity and the complexity of human language. The article concludes by highlighting the importance of effective text preprocessing in NLP projects and the continuous evolution of the field, which pushes the boundaries of machine understanding of human communication.

Introduction

Natural Language Processing (NLP) is a branch of artificial intelligence that strives to bridge the gap between human communication and machine understanding. By enabling machines to comprehend and respond to text and voice data, NLP powers various applications, from search engines like Google to conversational interfaces like Apple Siri and Google Assistant. In addition, NLP is integral to customer service chatbots, automated document processing, sentiment analysis, and machine translation tools like Google Translate.

Despite the significant progress in structured data processing, computers still need to work on dealing with unstructured data, particularly free-form text. Human language is inherently complex and nuanced, making it difficult for machines to interpret without advanced algorithms. NLP addresses this challenge by developing methods that allow computers to understand, analyse, and generate natural language.

Core Components of NLP

NLP has two main components: Natural Language Understanding (NLU) and Natural Language Generation (NLG). NLU enables machines to read, interpret, and summarise text, effectively allowing them to grasp the meaning and context of language. On the other hand, NLG will enable machines to generate coherent and contextually relevant text or speech, facilitating effective communication with humans.

For instance, when a user interacts with Google Assistant or Amazon Alexa, NLP technology enables these systems to understand the user's requests through NLU. NLG then allows the system to respond in a natural-sounding language that feels conversational and human-like.

Applications of NLP

NLP is applied across various domains, each requiring a different level of complexity and understanding. Here are some of the key applications.

1. **Text Classification**: Text classification involves categorising text into predefined categories based on content. It is widely used in spam detection, sentiment analysis, and news categorisation. For example, email systems use text classification to filter spam emails, while businesses use sentiment analysis to gauge customer opinions from social media or reviews.

2. **Sentiment Analysis**: Sentiment analysis, also known as opinion mining, classifies the underlying sentiment in a piece of text as positive, negative, or neutral. This is essential for businesses to understand customer responses, monitor brand reputation, and refine marketing strategies.

3. **Named Entity Recognition (NER)**: NER identifies and categorises named entities in text, such as people, organisations, and locations. It is crucial for tasks like content classification, information retrieval, and customer service automation.

4. **Machine Translation**: Machine translation converts text from one language to another. Popular tools include Google Translate and Microsoft Translator. While these tools are useful for quickly translating large volumes of text, they may need help with cultural nuances and contextual interpretations, sometimes producing robotic or culturally unaligned translations.

5. **Open-Domain Conversational Agents**: The most challenging NLP task involves creating open-domain conversational agents, such as Apple Siri or Amazon Alexa, capable of understanding and responding to any conversation across various topics. These agents handle multiple queries and provide meaningful interactions across diverse issues.

Challenges in NLP

Human language is a sophisticated communication system with complexities that pose significant challenges for NLP. One of the most difficult aspects of NLP is dealing with linguistic ambiguity—words and phrases often have multiple meanings depending on the context. For example, the sentences "man bit dog" and "dog bit man" are syntactically similar, but their meanings are vastly different. While humans can easily differentiate between the two, computers may struggle without additional contextual information.

Another challenge is the need for direct mapping between the vocabularies of different languages. This makes it difficult to transfer NLP solutions from one language to another, often requiring separate models and approaches for each language.

Importance of Text Preprocessing in NLP

Text preprocessing is a crucial step in any NLP project. It involves cleaning and transforming raw text into a format suitable for analysis and model building. Common preprocessing steps include case folding, punctuation removal, stopword elimination, and more advanced techniques like tokenisation, stemming, and lemmatisation.

Effective text preprocessing ensures the text data is clean, standardised, and ready for further analysis. By carefully selecting and applying preprocessing techniques, we can significantly enhance the performance of NLP models and achieve more accurate and meaningful results.

Conclusion

Natural Language Processing is a rapidly evolving field that continues to push the boundaries of what machines can achieve in understanding and replicating human communication. From search engines to virtual assistants, NLP powers many intelligent systems we interact with daily. However, the complexities of human language, including ambiguity and context, pose significant challenges for NLP systems.

As we develop more advanced NLP models, the ongoing challenge lies in encoding the vast amount of common knowledge humans take for granted into computational models. This effort is critical to improving the accuracy and reliability of NLP applications across different languages and contexts. By advancing our understanding of human language and refining NLP techniques, we can continue to enhance the capabilities of machines, making them more effective in understanding and generating natural language.

References

- Jurafsky, D., & Martin, J. H. (2008). Speech and Language Processing. ISBN: 978-0131873216
- Manning, C. D., Raghavan, P., & Schütze, H. (2008). Introduction to Information Retrieval. ISBN: 978-0521865715
- Pinker, S. (1994). The Language Instinct. ISBN: 978-0060976514

Additional Reading Material

- Bird, S., Klein, E., & Loper, E. (2009). Natural Language Processing with Python. ISBN: 978-0596516499
- Goldberg, Y. (2017). Neural Network Methods for Natural Language Processing. ISBN: 978-1627052986

- Liu, B. (2012). Sentiment Analysis and Opinion Mining. ISBN: 978-1608458844
- Russell, S., & Norvig, P. (2010). Artificial Intelligence: A Modern Approach. ISBN: 978-0136042594

140

Recommender Systems and Their Business Impact

Abstract

This article explores recommender systems, which have become essential in creating personalised user experiences across various industries. These systems predict user preferences to suggest the most suitable product, service, or content. The article delves into the different types of recommender systems, such as collaborative filtering, content-based, association rule-based, knowledge-based, and hybrid systems. It also discusses the technical challenges, such as the cold start problem, and the importance of security, privacy, and ethical considerations in developing these systems. The article highlights how recommender systems are built and refined through examples and demonstrations, ensuring they effectively cater to user needs. The discussion is aimed at both technical and non-technical audiences, offering insights into businesses' strategies to enhance customer satisfaction, sales growth, and long-term engagement.

Introduction

In today's digital age, businesses are increasingly focused on delivering personalised experiences to their customers. Recommender systems have emerged as a key technology enabling this personalisation by predicting user preferences and suggesting items—whether products, services, or content—that are most relevant to them. These systems have become integral to platforms like Netflix, Amazon, and Disney+, where they play a crucial role in enhancing user engagement, driving sales, and improving customer retention. This article explores the different types of recommender systems, their applications, the challenges involved in building them, and the ethical considerations that developers and businesses must consider.

Understanding Recommender Systems

Recommender systems are algorithms designed to suggest the most suitable items to users by predicting their preferences. These predictions are made by analysing various types of information, including interactions between users and items, the characteristics of the items themselves, and the behaviours of similar users. The goal is to create a personalised service that aligns closely with each user's interests, enhancing their overall experience and increasing their likelihood of continued engagement with the platform.

Recommender systems can be broadly classified into several types, each suited to different use cases and industries. The most common types include collaborative filtering, content-based filtering, association rule mining, knowledge-based systems, and hybrid systems that combine elements from the other types.

Types of Recommender Systems

Recommender systems have become integral to how we experience content and products online. They help users navigate vast amounts of information by suggesting items—whether products, services, or media content—that align with their preferences. These systems' effectiveness lies in the various methodologies used to generate recommendations, each tailored to different user needs and data types.

The recommender systems vary widely, from those that rely on user interactions and preferences to those that use sophisticated algorithms to identify patterns in data.

Understanding these different types of recommender systems is crucial for businesses and platforms aiming to deliver personalised and engaging user experiences. Each method has strengths and is suited to contexts, allowing for a tailored approach that meets diverse user needs. By leveraging the appropriate recommender system, businesses can enhance user satisfaction, drive engagement, and ultimately boost their bottom line.

Collaborative Filtering

Collaborative filtering is one of the most popular and widely implemented types of recommender systems. It works by finding patterns in user behaviour—specifically, by analysing users' preferences with similar interests. There are two main types of collaborative filtering.

- **User-Based Collaborative Filtering**: This method identifies users with similar preferences and recommends items that those users have liked. For example, if User A and User B rated certain movies highly, the system might recommend other movies that User B liked to User A.

- **Item-Based Collaborative Filtering**: Instead of focusing on similar users, item-based collaborative filtering looks for similarities between items. For instance, if a user has enjoyed Movie X, the system might recommend Movie Y if other users who liked Movie X also liked Movie Y.

Collaborative filtering is highly effective in environments with a rich history of user interaction data. Platforms like Amazon and Netflix extensively use collaborative filtering to suggest products and content users will likely enjoy based on their past behaviours and those of others with similar tastes.

Example: Netflix uses a sophisticated blend of user-based and item-based collaborative filtering to suggest movies and shows. By analysing users' viewing patterns with similar tastes, Netflix can recommend content that a user might not have discovered otherwise, thus enhancing the viewing experience and encouraging continued engagement.

Content-Based Filtering

Content-based filtering differs from collaborative filtering in that it does not rely on the preferences of other users. Instead, it focuses on the items' characteristics and the individual user's preferences. The system analyses the attributes of items a user has liked and recommends similar items.

This approach is particularly useful in scenarios with limited user interaction data, such as when a user is new to the platform. For example, when a new user signs up for Netflix, the platform may not have any data on their viewing history. To overcome this, Netflix asks users to rate a few movies or shows they have watched. Based on these ratings and the metadata associated with the content (e.g., genre, director, actors), Netflix can recommend similar content that aligns with the user's stated preferences.

Example: A user who frequently watches action movies on Netflix might be recommended other action movies with similar themes, directors, or actors. This approach ensures that the recommendations are relevant even if the user's interaction history is limited.

Association Rule Mining-Based Systems

Association rule mining is commonly used in market basket analysis to identify items frequently appearing together in transactions. This type of recommender system is particularly useful in retail environments where understanding product associations can drive sales strategies.

Association rule mining answers questions like "What items are often bought together?" By analysing large datasets of transactions, the system can identify patterns and recommend products that are likely to be purchased together. For instance, a grocery store might discover that customers who buy bread and butter are also expected to buy milk. This insight lets the store position these items together or offer them as a bundled deal, increasing sales.

Example: The famous, though debated, example of beer and diapers being frequently purchased together in supermarkets results from association rule mining. While the exact validity of this example is questionable, it illustrates how seemingly unrelated items can be associated based on transaction data.

Knowledge-Based Recommender Systems

Knowledge-based recommender systems are designed for rarely purchased items like real estate or luxury cars. In these cases, there isn't enough purchase history to use collaborative filtering or content-based methods effectively. Instead, a knowledge-based system relies on domain knowledge and user-specified criteria to make recommendations.

For example, a knowledge-based recommender might ask a user looking to buy a house about their preferred location, budget, and the number of bedrooms they want. Based on this information, the system recommends properties that meet the user's criteria. These recommendations are highly tailored to the user's needs, though they typically don't offer the element of surprise found in other types of recommender systems.

Example: A real estate website might use a knowledge-based recommender system to help users find properties based on specific requirements like location, price range, and amenities. The system uses domain knowledge to match user preferences with available properties, ensuring the recommendations are relevant and useful.

Hybrid Recommender Systems

Hybrid recommender systems combine multiple recommendation techniques to leverage each technique's strengths while mitigating weaknesses. By integrating collaborative filtering, content-based filtering, and other methods, hybrid systems can provide more accurate and versatile recommendations.

For instance, Netflix uses a hybrid model that first applies collaborative filtering to find users with similar preferences and then uses content-based filtering to recommend items identical to those liked by these users. This combination allows Netflix to provide highly personalised recommendations that are relevant and diverse, catering to a wide range of user preferences.

Example: Netflix's recommendation engine is a prime example of a hybrid recommender system. It combines collaborative filtering and content-based methods to ensure that users receive recommendations that align with their past behaviours while introducing them to new content they might not have discovered otherwise.

Challenges in Building Recommender Systems

Recommender systems have become a cornerstone of many online platforms, offering personalised suggestions that enhance user experience and drive engagement. However, developing and maintaining these systems involves navigating complex challenges that can significantly impact their effectiveness and the trust they inspire in users.

Understanding and addressing these challenges is essential for creating recommender systems that effectively deliver personalised content, safeguard user privacy, and promote a fair and inclusive online environment.

The Cold Start Problem

One of the most significant challenges in building recommender systems is the cold start problem. This issue arises when there is insufficient data about new users or items, making it difficult to provide reliable recommendations. For example, a new user on Netflix might need a viewing history for the system to analyse, or a new movie might need more ratings to be recommended confidently.

To mitigate this issue, platforms often use demographic information or initial user inputs, such as asking new users to rate a few movies or products, to generate initial recommendations. Over time, as more data is collected, the system becomes more adept at making accurate predictions.

Solution Example: Some platforms use a hybrid approach to overcome the cold start problem. For instance, they might combine demographic-based recommendations with content-based filtering until enough user interaction data is collected to apply collaborative filtering effectively.

Security and Privacy Concerns

Recommender systems collect vast amounts of user data, including both explicit data like ratings and implicit data like browsing behaviour. Ensuring this data is stored securely and used ethically is paramount. Compliance with regulations like the General Data Protection Regulation (GDPR) is necessary to maintain user trust and avoid legal complications.

Developers must also consider the ethical implications of their algorithms, particularly the potential for bias and the long-term effects of their recommendations on user behaviour. For example, a biased algorithm might disproportionately recommend content from certain genres or creators, limiting users' exposure to diverse content and perpetuating stereotypes.

Example: Platforms like Amazon have implemented strict data encryption and anonymisation techniques to protect user data while complying with GDPR and other privacy regulations. They also continuously monitor their recommendation algorithms to identify and mitigate potential biases.

Ethical Considerations in Recommender Systems

As recommender systems become increasingly prevalent across various digital platforms, the ethical implications of their design and implementation have come under greater scrutiny. While powerful in delivering personalised experiences, these systems also present significant ethical challenges that developers and companies must navigate. Two of the most pressing issues in this domain are algorithmic bias and the broader ethical dilemmas associated with personalisation.

Addressing these ethical challenges requires a thoughtful approach to algorithm design, data usage, and user transparency. By incorporating fairness-aware algorithms and offering users more control over their data, platforms can work towards creating recommender systems that are both effective and ethically sound.

Algorithmic Bias and Fairness

Algorithmic bias is a significant concern in the development of recommender systems. Bias can arise from the data used to train the algorithms or from the algorithms themselves, leading to recommendations that reinforce stereotypes or exclude certain groups. For instance, a music streaming service may favour popular artists over emerging ones, limiting the diversity of recommendations.

To address this issue, developers must design algorithms that promote fairness and diversity. This might involve techniques like fairness-aware machine learning or incorporating diverse datasets that reflect a wide range of user preferences.

Example: Spotify has implemented measures to ensure its recommendation engine promotes diverse artists, including emerging and lesser-known musicians. By diversifying the datasets and employing fairness-aware algorithms, Spotify can recommend a broader array of music to its users, thereby reducing bias and fostering a more inclusive listening experience.

Ethical Dilemmas in Personalisation

Another ethical consideration is the balance between personalisation and privacy. While personalised recommendations can significantly enhance user experience, they also raise concerns about how much personal data is collected and used. Users may only sometimes be aware of the extent to which their data is being analysed to generate recommendations, leading to potential privacy violations.

Transparency is key to navigating this ethical dilemma. Platforms should communicate how user data is collected, stored, and used. Providing users with control over their data, such as opting out of certain types of data collection or recommendation processes, can also help maintain trust.

Example: Netflix allows users to view and manage their viewing history, allowing them to control which data is used to inform future recommendations. This transparency helps users feel more in control of their personal information while enjoying personalised content's benefits.

Conclusion

Recommender systems are a powerful tool in the digital economy, driving personalisation, enhancing user experiences, and boosting business outcomes. By leveraging algorithms that analyse user behaviour and item characteristics, these systems can predict and suggest items users are most likely to appreciate, increasing engagement, sales, and customer retention.

However, building and maintaining effective recommender systems is challenging. The cold start problem, security and privacy concerns, and ethical considerations such as algorithmic bias and transparency must be carefully managed to ensure that these systems serve the best interests of both users and businesses.

As recommender systems evolve, the focus will likely shift toward creating more fair, transparent, and privacy-preserving algorithms. Businesses that successfully navigate these challenges will be well-positioned to offer superior personalised experiences that resonate with their users and foster long-term loyalty.

References

- Burke, R., Mobasher, B., & Zhang, J. (2013). Privacy-Preserving Recommender Systems: Challenges and Opportunities. ACM Transactions on Internet Technology (TOIT), 13(1), 1-26. DOI: https://doi.org/10.1145/2542182.2542191
- Jannach, D., Zanker, M., & Felfering, A. (2010). Recommender Systems: An Introduction. Cambridge University Press. ISBN: 978-0-521-49336-9

Additional Reading Material

- Aggarwal, C. C. (2016). Recommender Systems: The Textbook. Springer. ISBN: 978-3-319-29658-0
- Cosley, D., Lam, S. K., Albert, I., Konstan, J. A., & Riedl, J. (2003). Is seeing believing? How recommender system interfaces affect users' opinions. Proceedings of the SIGCHI Conference on Human Factors in Computing Systems. DOI: https://doi.org/10.1145/642611.642713
- Ricci, F., Rokach, L., & Shapira, B. (2015). Recommender Systems Handbook. Springer. ISBN: 978-1-4899-7637-6
- Schafer, J. B., Konstan, J. A., & Riedl, J. (2001). E-commerce recommendation applications. Data Mining and Knowledge Discovery, 5(1-2), 115-153. DOI: https://doi.org/10.1023/A:1009804230409

Case Studies of Successful AI Implementations

Abstract

This chapter presents a series of case studies highlighting the successful implementation of artificial intelligence (AI) and machine learning (ML) in various industries. It explores how leading companies like Netflix, Amazon, Google, IBM Watson, and Uber have leveraged AI/ML to revolutionise their operations, enhance customer satisfaction, and maintain market leadership. The case studies delve into the specific challenges these companies faced, the innovative solutions they developed using AI/ML, and the outcomes that have driven their success. By examining these real-world examples, the chapter underscores the transformative power of AI in diverse business contexts and offers valuable insights for organisations seeking to implement AI-driven strategies.

Introduction

The rapid advancement of artificial intelligence (AI) and machine learning (ML) has profoundly impacted various industries, enabling businesses to tackle complex challenges, optimise operations, and deliver personalised experiences to customers. From streaming services and e-commerce to search engines, healthcare, and ride-hailing, AI/ML has become a critical driver of innovation and competitive advantage.

This chapter explores how some of the world's most influential companies have successfully implemented AI and ML to address specific business challenges. Each case study provides a detailed look at how AI/ML technologies were integrated into the company's operations, the obstacles they overcame, and the measurable benefits they achieved. Through these examples, we aim to illustrate the broad potential of AI/ML and provide actionable insights for organisations looking to harness these technologies for their growth and success.

Netflix - Revolutionising Content Recommendation with Machine Learning

Netflix, the global streaming giant, has profoundly impacted how people consume entertainment by pioneering personalised content recommendations. Leveraging advanced machine learning algorithms, Netflix tailors its vast library of movies, TV shows, and documentaries to individual user preferences. This personalisation has enhanced user engagement and solidified Netflix's position as a dominant player in the highly competitive streaming industry.

The Challenge

In the early 2000s, Netflix transitioned from a DVD rental service to a streaming platform, offering its growing user base a vast array of content. As the library expanded, the challenge of ensuring users could easily discover content relevant to their tastes became increasingly complex. Traditional content browsing methods needed to be more sufficient to handle the scale and diversity of Netflix's offerings, leading to potential user frustration and disengagement.

Netflix recognised that its success hinged on its ability to keep users engaged by offering content resonating with their preferences. The challenge was to develop a system that could accurately predict and recommend content that each user would find appealing, thereby improving user retention and increasing the time spent on the platform.

The Solution

To tackle this challenge, Netflix developed a sophisticated recommendation system based on collaborative filtering. This machine-learning technique leverages user behaviour data to predict what content a user might enjoy.

Collaborative Filtering

Initially, Netflix experimented with **user-based collaborative filtering**, where the system recommends content based on the viewing habits of similar users. For example, if User A and User B have similar viewing histories, the system might recommend content watched by User A to User B and vice versa. However, as the user base grew, this approach became computationally intensive and less scalable.

Netflix shifted to **item-based collaborative filtering** to overcome scalability issues. This method focuses on the relationships between different content items rather than users. The algorithm identifies items (e.g., movies or shows) frequently watched together or rated similarly and recommends them to users based on their viewing history. For example, if a user watches "Stranger Things," the system might recommend "The Haunting of Hill House" based on patterns observed across the platform.

Matrix Factorisation

In 2006, Netflix introduced a prize competition known as the Netflix Prize, which offered $1 million to the team that could significantly improve its recommendation algorithm. The winning solution employed matrix factorisation, which decomposes the large matrix of user-item interactions into smaller matrices that capture latent factors, such as genres or themes, influencing user preferences. This method improved recommendation accuracy by identifying underlying patterns in the data that were not immediately obvious.

Personalisation at Scale

Beyond collaborative filtering, Netflix's recommendation system has evolved to incorporate a blend of algorithms, including deep learning models and natural language processing (NLP). These models analyse user interactions, such as viewing history, search queries, and even the timing of content consumption, to refine recommendations. Moreover, Netflix personalises the content and the presentation, including the thumbnails displayed to users, which are tailored based on what might appeal most to each individual.

Continuous Learning and Feedback Loops

Netflix continuously refines its recommendation system through A/B testing and real-time feedback loops. By experimenting with different algorithms and user interfaces, Netflix gathers data on what drives engagement and fine-tunes its models accordingly. This iterative approach ensures that the recommendation system adapts to changing user behaviours and preferences, maintaining its relevance over time.

The Outcome

The implementation of a robust machine learning-powered recommendation system has had a profound impact on Netflix's business. The personalised recommendations have led to a significant increase in user satisfaction, as subscribers are more likely to find content they enjoy, thus spending more time on the platform.

Increased User Engagement

Personalised recommendations have drastically reduced users' time searching for content, leading to longer viewing sessions and higher overall user engagement. The system's ability to surface relevant content has also contributed to the "binge-watching" phenomenon, where users consume multiple episodes or movies in one sitting, further boosting watch time.

Enhanced User Retention

By consistently delivering content that aligns with user preferences, Netflix has seen improvements in user retention rates. Satisfied users are less likely to cancel their subscriptions, contributing to the platform's steady growth in subscriber numbers.

Data-Driven Content Creation:

The insights from user interaction data have also influenced Netflix's content creation strategy. By understanding what types of content resonate with different segments of its audience, Netflix can make more informed decisions about which shows and movies to produce or acquire. This data-driven approach has created original content highly tailored to user preferences, such as the critically acclaimed series "House of Cards" and "Stranger Things."

Market Leadership:

Netflix's success in leveraging machine learning for content recommendation has been a key factor in its rise to the top of the streaming industry. The platform's ability to deliver a personalised experience has set it apart from competitors, helping it maintain a loyal subscriber base and attract new users in a crowded market.

Conclusion

Netflix's innovative use of machine learning in its recommendation system has revolutionised how content is delivered to users, setting a new standard for personalisation in the entertainment industry. This approach's success highlights the transformative power of machine learning in enhancing user experience, driving engagement, and achieving business objectives. As Netflix continues to evolve its recommendation algorithms, it remains at the forefront of innovation, shaping the future of streaming entertainment.

Amazon - Optimising Supply Chain with Machine Learning

Amazon, one of the world's largest e-commerce companies, operates a highly complex supply chain network across the globe. With millions of products available and billions of transactions processed annually, managing this supply chain efficiently is crucial to Amazon's success. To maintain its competitive edge, Amazon has integrated machine learning into various aspects of its supply chain management, enabling the company to forecast demand more accurately, manage inventory more effectively, and optimise delivery routes. This case study explores how these machine learning implementations have transformed Amazon's supply chain operations, significantly improving efficiency, cost reduction, and customer satisfaction.

The Challenge

Amazon's supply chain is an intricate web of suppliers, warehouses, distribution centres, and delivery routes that must work seamlessly together to ensure the timely delivery of products to customers. The scale and complexity of this operation present several challenges.

- **Demand Forecasting**: Accurately predicting customer demand is critical to avoid overstocking or stockouts. With millions of products across various

categories, each with its demand patterns, this task becomes exponentially difficult.
- **Inventory Management**: Ensuring that the right amount of inventory is available at the right locations is crucial for meeting customer expectations. Poor inventory management can lead to excess inventory costs or missed sales opportunities.
- **Logistics and Route Optimisation**: Delivering millions of packages efficiently requires optimising delivery routes and logistics operations to minimise costs and meet delivery timelines. As Amazon expands its logistics network, route optimisation becomes more complex.

The Solution

Amazon has implemented machine learning models to address these challenges across various aspects of its supply chain. These models analyse vast amounts of data, learn from historical trends, and make predictions that help optimise operations.

Demand Forecasting

Amazon uses machine learning algorithms to analyse historical sales data, customer behaviour, seasonal trends, and external factors such as economic conditions and weather patterns to predict future demand for each product. These models continuously learn from new data, allowing them to adapt to changing trends and improve accuracy over time.

Amazon's dynamic forecasting models can be adjusted based on real-time data. For instance, during major sales events like Prime Day or Black Friday, these models help Amazon anticipate spikes in demand and adjust inventory levels accordingly.

Inventory Management

Machine learning models determine optimal inventory levels at various fulfilment centres. These models consider lead times, supplier reliability, and shipping costs to automate inventory replenishment decisions. Amazon reduces the likelihood of stockouts and overstock situations by ensuring that inventory is in the right place at the right time.

To further enhance efficiency, Amazon uses machine learning to optimise inventory placement across its global network of fulfilment centres. The models predict where demand will likely occur and ensure that inventory is positioned close to customers, reducing shipping times and costs.

Logistics and Route Optimisation

Amazon's machine learning models are crucial in optimising delivery routes for its vast logistics network, including its last-mile delivery operations. These models analyse traffic patterns, delivery locations, and package volumes to generate the most efficient delivery routes for drivers. This reduces fuel consumption and delivery times and enhances the logistics network's efficiency.

The models can adjust routes in real time based on changing conditions, such as traffic congestion or weather disruptions. This agility ensures that deliveries remain on schedule and resources are used efficiently.

As Amazon explores drone delivery through its Prime Air initiative, machine learning is used to optimise flight paths, assess environmental conditions, and ensure the safety and efficiency of drone operations.

The Outcome

Integrating machine learning into Amazon's supply chain operations has yielded significant benefits.

Increased Operational Efficiency

Amazon has greatly enhanced its operational efficiency by automating and optimising various aspects of its supply chain. Machine learning-driven demand forecasting and inventory management ensure that products are always available where and when needed, minimising delays and improving order fulfilment speed.

Cost Reduction

Machine learning has enabled Amazon to reduce costs in several ways. Improved demand forecasting reduces excess inventory, lowering storage costs. Optimised inventory placement minimises shipping distances and times, reducing logistics expenses. Additionally, route optimisation lowers fuel consumption and vehicle wear and tear, contributing to further cost savings.

Enhanced Customer Satisfaction

Timely and accurate order fulfilment is a cornerstone of Amazon's customer experience. By leveraging machine learning to predict demand, manage inventory, and optimise delivery routes, Amazon ensures that customers receive their orders quickly and reliably. This consistency in service quality has helped Amazon maintain high customer satisfaction and loyalty.

Scalability and Innovation

The scalability of machine learning models has allowed Amazon to continuously expand its product offerings and geographic reach without compromising operational efficiency. Moreover, the insights gained from these models have driven innovation, such as developing new delivery methods and enhancing the customer experience.

Conclusion

Amazon's use of machine learning to optimise its supply chain exemplifies the transformative impact of AI on modern business operations. By addressing the complexities of demand forecasting, inventory management, and logistics, Amazon has improved its operational efficiency, reduced costs and significantly enhanced its ability to meet and exceed customer expectations. This case study underscores the potential of machine learning to revolutionise supply chain management and provides valuable lessons for other organisations looking to leverage AI in their operations.

Google - Enhancing Search Engine Performance with Deep Learning

Google's search engine is one of the most widely used and essential tools in the digital world, serving billions of queries daily. The quality of search results directly impacts user satisfaction and, consequently, Google's revenue from advertising. To maintain its leadership in the search engine market, Google has continually refined its algorithms, integrating advanced deep learning techniques to understand better and rank search queries. This case study explores how Google's implementation of deep learning, particularly through its RankBrain algorithm, has significantly improved the accuracy and relevance of search results, ensuring a superior user experience.

The Challenge

Google's primary challenge is to deliver accurate and relevant search results for a vast array of user queries, which vary in complexity, language, and intent. Some of the key challenges include the following.

Understanding User Intent

Users often input queries that are ambiguous, misspelt, or phrased in unconventional ways. The challenge lies in understanding the true intent behind these queries and delivering results that match the user's expectations.

For example, searching for "apple" could refer to a fruit, a technology company, or a music label. Google needs to determine the most likely intent based on contextual clues.

Processing Natural Language

Natural language processing (NLP) is critical for understanding the nuances of human language, including synonyms, idioms, and regional dialects. The search engine must decipher the meaning behind complex queries and retrieve the most relevant results.

Users increasingly rely on voice search, which often involves more conversational language, so the need for sophisticated NLP capabilities has grown.

Handling Long-Tail Queries

Long-tail queries are highly specific and less common search phrases that can be difficult to interpret and match with relevant content. They require a deep understanding of language and context to deliver precise results.

For example, a query like "best eco-friendly smartphone case for iPhone 12 under $20" is very specific and involves multiple criteria that must be considered simultaneously.

Ranking Search Results

Once the search engine understands the query, it must rank the results based on relevance, authority, and user satisfaction. With millions of web pages to consider, this ranking process is complex and computationally intensive.

Google aims to provide the most relevant results and rank them based on what users are most likely to find useful and engaging.

The Solution

To address these challenges, Google has integrated deep learning models into its search engine algorithms, most notably with the introduction of RankBrain in 2015. RankBrain is a machine learning-based component of Google's search algorithm that processes and interprets search queries to deliver more relevant results.

RankBrain: A Revolutionary Search Algorithm

RankBrain is a deep learning system that uses artificial intelligence to help Google process search queries. It is particularly effective at handling queries that Google has never seen before, which make up a significant portion of daily searches.

RankBrain uses machine learning to convert written language into mathematical vectors that the algorithm can understand. It then analyses past searches to find patterns to help predict the most relevant results for new queries. For example, if a user searches for "best running shoes for flat feet," RankBrain can understand that "flat feet" is a critical attribute and prioritise search results that mention this feature.

RankBrain continuously learns and adapts to new data. By analysing the success of past search results, it fine-tunes its understanding of language and user behaviour, ensuring that it delivers increasingly accurate and relevant results over time.

Natural Language Processing (NLP) and BERT

In 2019, Google introduced BERT (Bidirectional Encoder Representations from Transformers), another deep learning model that significantly improved the search engine's ability to understand the context of words in a query. Unlike traditional models that process words in a query one at a time, BERT considers the full context of a word by looking at the words that come before and after it, which is especially useful for understanding the nuances of longer and more complex queries.

BERT allows Google to understand queries more human-likely, particularly for longer, conversational, or context-heavy queries. For instance, in the query "2019 Brazil traveller to the USA needs a visa," BERT helps Google understand that the user is a Brazilian traveller asking about visa requirements rather than searching for general information about visas.

Handling Ambiguity and Context with Deep Learning

Google's deep learning models are designed to handle ambiguous queries by considering multiple possible meanings and ranking the results based on what users in similar situations have found useful. For example, if many users who searched for "apple" clicked on links related to the tech company rather than the fruit, RankBrain would prioritise tech-related results for similar future queries.

Deep learning also enables Google to understand better the context in which a query is made. For instance, if a user searches for "best restaurants near me" while using a mobile device, Google's algorithms can factor in the user's location, time of day, and even previous dining preferences to provide the most relevant results.

Enhancing User Experience with Personalised Search Results

Google's deep learning models personalise search results based on a user's search history, location, and preferences. This means that two users searching for the same term might see different results tailored to their needs and past behaviour.

Google's algorithms can adjust search results based on current events, trending topics, and user behaviour patterns. For example, if a major news story breaks, Google can quickly update its search results to prioritise the most relevant and recent information.

The Outcome

Integrating deep learning into Google's search engine has profoundly impacted search results' accuracy, relevance, and user experience.

Increased Accuracy and Relevance

Deep learning models like RankBrain and BERT have dramatically improved Google's ability to understand and process complex queries. This has led to more accurate search results, particularly for ambiguous, rare, or context-dependent queries.

Improved User Satisfaction

By delivering more relevant and personalised search results, Google has enhanced the overall user experience. Users are more likely to find what they seek quickly, reducing the need to refine or repeat searches. This satisfaction translates into continued user loyalty and increased usage.

Maintained Market Leadership

Google's ongoing innovation in search technology, driven by deep learning, has allowed it to maintain its dominant position in the search engine market. The continuous refinement of search algorithms ensures that Google remains ahead of competitors, offering a search experience that is difficult to match.

Real-Time Responsiveness

Google's ability to adjust search results based on emerging trends and current events ensures users receive the most up-to-date and relevant information. This capability is particularly important for news-related queries and rapidly changing topics.

Conclusion

Google's strategic integration of deep learning into its search engine operations significantly advances how search queries are processed and ranked. By focusing on understanding user intent, processing natural language, and delivering personalised search experiences, Google has enhanced the accuracy and relevance of its search results and set a high standard in the industry. These deep learning implementations' success underscores AI's transformative power in creating superior user experiences and maintaining competitive advantage in the digital marketplace.

IBM Watson - Transforming Healthcare with AI and Machine Learning

IBM Watson, a powerful AI and machine learning platform, has made significant contributions to the healthcare sector by transforming how medical professionals diagnose diseases, personalise treatment plans, and conduct research. With its ability to analyse vast amounts of medical data, Watson has revolutionised the healthcare industry, offering tools that assist clinicians in making more accurate diagnoses, tailoring treatments to individual patients, and accelerating medical research. This case study examines how IBM Watson has addressed key challenges in healthcare and the outcomes that have emerged from its implementation.

The Challenge

Healthcare is a field characterised by vast amounts of data, ranging from patient records and diagnostic images to research papers and clinical trial results. Despite the availability of this information, healthcare professionals often need help.

Complexity of Diagnoses

Diagnosing diseases, particularly complex and rare conditions, requires analysing various data sources, including patient history, lab results, imaging studies, and genetic information. Despite their expertise, human clinicians can need help with this data's sheer volume and complexity, leading to potential misdiagnoses or delays in diagnosis.

Personalisation of Treatment Plans

Each patient is unique, and effective treatment often requires a personalised approach that considers an individual's genetic makeup, lifestyle, and other factors. Developing personalised treatment plans is a time-consuming process that requires analysing multiple data points and staying current with the latest medical research.

Accelerating Medical Research

Medical research is accelerating, with thousands of new research papers published annually. However, integrating these findings into clinical practice can take time and effort. Researchers need tools to sift through vast amounts of data to identify relevant insights quickly.

The Solution

IBM Watson addresses these challenges by deploying advanced AI and machine learning models to analyse medical data, provide clinical decision support, and accelerate research.

Watson for Oncology

Watson for Oncology is a cognitive computing system designed to assist oncologists in developing personalised cancer treatment plans. It analyses structured and unstructured data from various sources, including patient records, clinical guidelines, medical literature, and research data.

Watson for Oncology processes a patient's medical data, including genetic information, and cross-references it with a vast corpus of medical literature and treatment guidelines. The system then provides oncologists with evidence-based treatment options ranked by their potential efficacy and supporting information from the literature. This allows clinicians to consider the latest research and treatment options.

Using Watson for Oncology has led to more informed treatment decisions, especially in complex cases with multiple treatment options. It has helped reduce the time required to develop treatment plans and has ensured that patients receive the most current and effective care possible.

Watson for Genomics

Watson for Genomics is designed to interpret genomic data, helping clinicians understand the genetic factors contributing to a patient's disease. This is particularly important in cancer care, where genetic mutations can guide treatment decisions.

Watson for Genomics analyses a patient's genetic data and identifies mutations that may drive the disease. It then correlates these mutations with relevant clinical trials, drugs, and research studies, providing oncologists with actionable insights that can personalise treatment.

By offering insights into the genetic drivers of disease, Watson for Genomics enables clinicians to tailor treatments to each patient's genetic profile. This personalised approach has led to more effective treatments and improved patient outcomes, particularly in cases where standard therapies have failed.

Watson for Clinical Trial Matching

Identifying eligible patients for clinical trials is a significant challenge in medical research. Watson for Clinical Trial Matching streamlines this process by analysing patient data to identify potential matches for ongoing trials.

Watson for Clinical Trial Matching scans patient records to identify individuals who meet the criteria for participation in clinical trials. It cross-references patient data with trial protocols to suggest eligible candidates, thus speeding up the recruitment process and helping researchers find participants more efficiently.

This tool has accelerated the process of matching patients with relevant clinical trials, increasing participation rates and helping to bring new treatments to market faster. It also ensures that patients have access to cutting-edge therapies that might not be available.

Accelerating Medical Research

Watson has assisted researchers in analysing vast scientific literature. For example, Watson has been used to identify potential drug candidates by sifting through thousands of research papers, clinical trial results, and patient records. It can identify patterns and connections that might not be immediately apparent to human researchers.

Watson's ability to process and analyse massive datasets has accelerated medical research discovery. It has helped identify new drug targets, repurpose existing medications, and develop novel therapies, contributing to faster research breakthroughs and the advancement of medical knowledge.

The Outcome

Integrating IBM Watson into healthcare has yielded significant benefits, transforming how clinicians diagnose and treat patients and how researchers conduct medical studies.

Improved Patient Outcomes

Watson's ability to analyse complex datasets and provide evidence-based recommendations has led to more accurate diagnoses and personalised treatment plans. As a result, patients receive care better tailored to their specific conditions, leading to improved outcomes, especially in cases of complex or rare diseases.

Faster Research Breakthroughs

By accelerating the identification of relevant research insights and clinical trial matches, Watson has shortened the time required to bring new treatments from the lab to the clinic. This has been particularly impactful in fields such as oncology, where rapid advancements in treatment options can save lives.

Enhanced Decision-Making in Medical Practices

Watson's clinical decision support tools provide clinicians access to the latest medical research and guidelines, enabling them to make more informed decisions. This support is particularly valuable in complex cases where multiple treatment options are available, helping to ensure that patients receive the best possible care.

Increased Efficiency in Clinical Trials

By automating the process of matching patients with clinical trials, Watson has made it easier for researchers to find eligible participants, thus speeding up the recruitment process. This efficiency has helped increase participation rates in clinical trials, leading to quicker and more successful studies.

Conclusion

IBM Watson has played a pivotal role in transforming healthcare by applying AI and machine learning to some of the most pressing challenges in the field. Watson has enhanced patient outcomes and advanced healthcare professionals' capabilities by improving diagnosis accuracy, personalising treatment plans, and accelerating research. As AI continues to evolve, tools like IBM Watson will likely play an increasingly important role in shaping the future of medicine, driving further innovation, and improving the quality of care for patients worldwide.

Uber - Using Machine Learning to Enhance Ride-Hailing Services

Uber, one of the world's leading ride-hailing companies, operates in a highly competitive market where success depends on efficiently matching drivers with riders, setting optimal pricing, and accurately predicting demand. Uber has deeply integrated machine learning into its platform to maintain its competitive edge, optimising pricing strategies, forecasting demand, and improving overall user experience. This case study explores how Uber leverages machine learning to manage the complexities of real-time operations, balancing supply and demand and enhancing the service quality for drivers and riders.

The Challenge

Operating a global ride-hailing service presents several significant challenges, especially in managing the dynamic nature of supply (available drivers) and demand (riders needing rides). Some of the key challenges include the following.

Dynamic Supply and Demand

Demand for rides fluctuates throughout the day, influenced by time, weather, local events, and holidays. Simultaneously, drivers' availability varies as they log in and out of the app. Uber must dynamically balance this supply and demand to minimise wait times for riders and ensure drivers can maximise their earnings.

Real-Time Pricing Optimisation

To manage fluctuations in demand, Uber employs dynamic pricing (often called "surge pricing"), where prices increase during peak demand periods to attract more drivers to areas with high rider demand. Setting these real-time prices to optimise the balance between rider affordability and driver incentive is challenging.

Driver-Partner Matching

Efficiently matching riders with the nearest available drivers minimises wait times and ensures a seamless experience. While operating in real-time, this matching process must account for the driver's location, traffic conditions, and rider preferences.

Predicting Demand

Accurately predicting where and when demand will spike is essential for positioning drivers in the right areas before the demand materialises. This requires analysing vast amounts of real-time data to forecast short-term and long-term demand patterns.

The Solution

Uber has developed and deployed a suite of machine-learning algorithms designed to address these challenges, enhancing the efficiency of its operations and improving the user experience for riders and drivers.

Dynamic Pricing (Surge Pricing)

Uber's dynamic pricing model adjusts ride prices in real-time based on current market conditions. Machine learning algorithms analyse demand, driver availability, traffic conditions, and external factors like weather or events. When demand exceeds supply, prices increase to encourage more drivers to move to high-demand areas, ensuring that riders can still get a ride despite the surge in demand.

Dynamic pricing helps Uber efficiently manage peak demand periods, ensuring that riders can still access rides, albeit at a higher cost, while drivers are incentivised to meet the increased demand. This balance helps minimise wait times for riders and maximises earnings for drivers, contributing to overall platform efficiency.

Demand Prediction

Uber's demand prediction algorithms leverage historical ride data, weather patterns, time of day, day of the week, and local events to forecast where and when ride demand will likely increase. These predictions allow Uber to proactively manage driver availability by sending alerts or notifications to drivers, suggesting where they should position themselves to maximise their chances of getting ride requests.

By accurately predicting demand, Uber can ensure that drivers are available in the right locations at the right times, reducing the likelihood of riders experiencing long wait times or difficulty finding a ride. This proactive approach improves rider

satisfaction and helps drivers optimise their earnings.

Driver-Partner Matching

Uber's machine learning algorithms analyse real-time data on driver locations, traffic conditions, and rider locations to optimise the matching process. The system considers multiple factors, such as the distance between the driver and rider, the driver's current trajectory, and the estimated arrival time. The goal is to minimise wait times for riders while ensuring that drivers can complete trips efficiently.

Efficient driver-partner matching reduces idle time for drivers and wait times for riders, leading to a smoother, faster, and more satisfying experience for both parties. This optimisation contributes to Uber's reliability and quick service reputation, helping maintain customer loyalty.

Improving User Experience with Personalisation

Uber also uses machine learning to personalise the user experience. For example, the app can suggest frequently visited destinations, recommend the best time to request a ride based on traffic patterns, or offer personalised pricing incentives to encourage repeat usage. These features are powered by algorithms that analyse individual user behaviour and preferences.

Personalised experiences help Uber enhance user satisfaction, encouraging loyalty and repeat business. By tailoring the service to individual preferences, Uber ensures that the platform meets the specific needs of each user, whether they are frequent riders or occasional users.

The Outcome

Applying machine learning across Uber's operations has resulted in several significant benefits, helping the company maintain its leadership in the competitive ride-hailing market.

Increased Operational Efficiency

By optimising dynamic pricing, demand prediction, and driver-partner matching, Uber has streamlined its operations, reduced inefficiencies, and ensured that resources are allocated where they are needed most. This operational efficiency is critical in a market where profit margins can be thin and competition fierce.

Improved Customer Satisfaction

Machine learning has enabled Uber to reduce wait times, ensure ride availability even during peak periods, and offer a more personalised experience. These improvements have led to higher customer satisfaction, with riders appreciating the reliability and responsiveness of the service.

Maximised Driver Earnings

For drivers, machine learning algorithms help maximise earnings by guiding them to high-demand areas and optimising their routes to minimise downtime. This enhances driver satisfaction and helps retain drivers on the platform, essential for sustaining the service.

Sustained Market Leadership

Uber's ability to leverage machine learning for real-time decision-making has been a key factor in maintaining its dominance in the ride-hailing industry. By continuously improving the user experience and operational efficiency, Uber has stayed ahead of competitors and maintained its position as a leading global ride-hailing platform.

Conclusion

Uber's integration of machine learning into its core operations illustrates the transformative power of AI in managing complex, real-time services. By addressing the challenges of dynamic supply and demand, real-time pricing, and efficient driver-partner matching, Uber has optimised its operations and enhanced the experience for both riders and drivers. The success of these machine learning implementations underscores their importance in maintaining Uber's competitive edge and demonstrates the broader potential of AI to revolutionise service-based industries.

References

- Amatriain, X., & Basilico, J. (2012). Netflix Recommendations: Beyond the 5 stars (Part 1). https://netflixtechblog.com/netflix-

recommendations-beyond-the-5-stars-part-1-55838468f429
- Chen, L., Mislove, A., & Wilson, C. (2015). Peeking Beneath the Hood of Uber. In Proceedings of the 2015 ACM Conference on Internet Measurement Conference (pp. 495-508). DOI: https://doi.org/10.1145/2815675.2815681
- Dean, J., & Corrado, G. (2015). Large Scale Deep Learning for Intelligent Computer Systems. Communications of the ACM, 58(4), 56-65. DOI: https://doi.org/10.1145/2699415
- Koren, Y., Bell, R., & Volinsky, C. (2009). Matrix Factorization Techniques for Recommender Systems. IEEE Computer, 42(8), 30-37. DOI: https://doi.org/10.1109/MC.2009.263
- Tomsett, R., & Preece, A. (2019). Watson for Genomics: Machine Learning for Precision Medicine. IBM Journal of Research and Development, 63(6), 1-7. DOI: https://doi.org/10.1147/JRD.2019.2952073
- Topol, E. (2019). High-performance medicine: the convergence of human and artificial intelligence. Nature Medicine, 25,

44-56. DOI: https://doi.org/10.1038/s41591-018-0300-7

Additional Reading Material

- Daugherty, P. R., & Wilson, H. J. (2018). Human + Machine: Reimagining Work in the Age of AI. Harvard Business Review Press. ISBN: 978-1633693869
- Goodfellow, I., Bengio, Y., & Courville, A. (2016). Deep Learning. MIT Press. ISBN: 978-0262035613
- Jannach, D., Zanker, M., Felfernig, A., & Friedrich, G. (2011). Recommender Systems: An Introduction. Cambridge University Press. ISBN: 978-0521493369
- Kuhn, M., & Johnson, K. (2013). Applied Predictive Modeling. Springer. ISBN: 978-1461468486
- Mitchell, M. (2019). Artificial Intelligence: A Guide for Thinking Humans. Penguin. ISBN: 978-0241404829

Case Studies of Failed AI Implementations

Abstract

This chapter examines three failed AI implementations case studies—Microsoft's Tay chatbot, Amazon's AI recruitment tool, and Google Photos' image recognition system. Each case highlights significant shortcomings in AI development, including unsupervised learning without adequate safeguards, biases in training data, and insufficient testing across diverse demographics. These failures resulted in public backlash, reputational damage, and a broader erosion of trust in AI technologies. The chapter analyses these cases and underscores the importance of ethical considerations, diverse training datasets, rigorous testing, and transparency in AI development. The lessons learned from these incidents provide crucial insights for building more inclusive and reliable AI systems in the future.

Introduction

Artificial Intelligence (AI) has the potential to transform industries, improve efficiencies, and offer innovative solutions to complex problems. However, the development and deployment of AI systems are fraught with challenges, particularly when ethical considerations and fairness are not adequately addressed. When AI fails, the consequences can be significant, not only in terms of technical setbacks but also in the social and ethical implications. The following case studies of Microsoft's Tay chatbot, Amazon's AI recruitment tool, and Google Photos' image recognition system serve as cautionary tales. Each case illustrates how biases in training data, inadequate testing, and a lack of oversight can lead to AI systems that perpetuate harm and reinforce inequalities. By exploring these failures, we can better understand the critical importance of developing AI that is fair, transparent, and accountable.

Microsoft Tay - The Chatbot That Went Rogue

In March 2016, Microsoft introduced Tay, an AI-powered Twitter chatbot designed to engage in conversations with users and learn from those interactions. Tay was built using natural language processing (NLP) techniques and was intended to mimic the conversational patterns of a teenage girl, making it relatable to young social media users. Microsoft envisioned Tay as a showcase of how AI could engage with the public, learn from social interactions, and improve its conversational abilities over time. However, within 24 hours of its launch, Tay began posting offensive, racist, and inappropriate tweets, forcing Microsoft to shut down the chatbot and issue public apologies.

Failure Points

The rapid failure of Microsoft's Tay chatbot is a critical example of the potential pitfalls in deploying AI systems in uncontrolled public environments. Although intended to showcase conversational AI, Tay quickly became a cautionary tale due to several significant oversights.

Understanding these failure points is crucial for anyone involved in AI development. This analysis highlights the complexities and responsibilities of creating AI that interacts safely and effectively with the public.

Unsupervised Learning

Tay was designed to learn from user interactions on Twitter without sufficient safeguards or filters to prevent harmful content absorption. The chatbot used a form of unsupervised learning, analysing and responding to tweets in real time, learning from the patterns and language it encountered. However, this approach made Tay vulnerable to manipulation. Malicious users quickly exploited this flaw, flooding Tay with offensive content that it began incorporating into its tweets.

Unlike supervised learning models trained on carefully curated datasets, Tay's learning process was unmonitored, allowing it to adopt and amplify the offensive language it encountered. This lack of filtering mechanisms to detect and block harmful input resulted in the chatbot producing highly inappropriate content.

Inadequate Testing

Before launching Tay, Microsoft conducted limited testing in controlled environments where the chatbot interacted with pre-approved inputs. However, this testing could have adequately simulated the chaotic and unpredictable nature of a public platform like Twitter, where users can post anything without moderation.

The testing phase failed to account for the possibility that users might intentionally provoke the chatbot or manipulate its responses. This oversight in anticipating and safeguarding against potential misuse was a critical failure in the development and deployment process.

Reputational Damage

The rapid degeneration of Tay's interactions into offensive and inappropriate territory led to widespread public criticism. Media outlets and social media users quickly highlighted the incident as a failure of AI ethics and responsibility. The backlash was directed at Tay and Microsoft, criticised for their lack of foresight and responsibility in deploying such a system without adequate safeguards.

Microsoft was forced to shut down Tay within 24 hours of its launch and issue public apologies, acknowledging the failure and committing to better oversight in future AI projects. The incident temporarily damaged Microsoft's reputation, particularly in the AI community, where ethical AI development is paramount.

Lessons Learned

The fallout from Microsoft's Tay chatbot highlighted critical areas where AI development and deployment practices must evolve. The incident underscored the necessity of implementing robust safeguards and ethical considerations in AI systems, particularly those designed to interact with the public in real-time.

The Need for Robust Moderation and Content Filtering Systems

One key lesson from the Tay incident is incorporating robust moderation and content-filtering mechanisms in AI systems that interact with the public. These systems should be designed to detect and block harmful or inappropriate content before the AI can process or reproduce it. This could involve integrating supervised learning components or human-in-the-loop systems where human moderators review and filter the content the AI encounters.

Developers must prioritise ethical considerations in AI design, particularly when deploying systems that learn from user interactions in real-time. This includes establishing clear guidelines for acceptable input and ensuring the AI adheres to these guidelines.

Importance of Simulating Real-World Environments During Testing

AI systems intended for public interaction should undergo rigorous testing in environments that closely mimic real-world conditions. This includes exposing the AI to various inputs, including potential misuse scenarios, to assess how it will respond. Testing should focus on technical performance and ethical and social implications.

Developers need to anticipate how users might attempt to exploit or manipulate AI systems and design countermeasures accordingly. This proactive approach can help mitigate risks and prevent incidents like the Tay debacle.

Necessity of Continuous Monitoring and Human Oversight

Even after deployment, AI systems should be continuously monitored to ensure they behave as intended. This includes real-time monitoring of the AI's interactions and outputs, with mechanisms to intervene if the system produces inappropriate or harmful content.

AI systems that learn from user interactions should only operate partially autonomously. Human oversight is crucial to reviewing the AI's learning process, intervening when necessary, and guiding the AI's development to ensure it aligns with ethical standards and user expectations.

Conclusion

The failure of Microsoft's Tay chatbot serves as a cautionary tale about the risks of deploying AI systems that interact with the public without adequate safeguards, testing, and oversight. The incident highlighted the importance of ethical considerations in AI development, the need for robust content moderation, and the value of comprehensive testing in real-world scenarios. By learning from Tay's failure, developers can better understand the complexities of creating AI that interacts safely and responsibly with users, helping to prevent similar incidents in the future.

Amazon's AI Recruitment Tool - Bias in Hiring

In its ongoing efforts to innovate and streamline business processes, Amazon developed an AI-based recruitment tool designed to automate the initial screening of resumes. The tool was intended to help the company efficiently identify top candidates by analysing resumes and assigning scores to applicants based on their qualifications. However, it was later discovered that the tool exhibited significant bias against female candidates, consistently favouring resumes that used predominantly male-associated language and penalising those with terms associated with female applicants. This revelation highlighted serious flaws in developing and deploying AI systems, particularly in sensitive areas like recruitment, where fairness and equity are paramount.

Failure Points

The development and deployment of Amazon's AI recruitment tool revealed significant flaws that compromised the system's fairness and effectiveness. Although intended to streamline the hiring process by automating the initial screening of resumes, the tool perpetuated and amplified existing biases within the industry.

By examining these critical failure points, we can better understand how AI systems, when not carefully managed and ethically guided, can inadvertently reinforce inequalities rather than mitigate them.

Training Data Bias

The AI recruitment tool was trained on a decade's resumes submitted to Amazon, during which the tech industry was predominantly male-dominated. As a result, the training data reflected this imbalance, with most successful candidates being men. The AI learned patterns from this biased dataset, associating successful hires with male-dominated roles and language.

Because the training data was biased, the AI model began to favour resumes that mirrored those of past male applicants, effectively penalising resumes with indicators of female involvement, such as mentions of women's organisations or female-associated activities. For example, a resume listing "women's chess club captain" might be ranked lower than one with similar experience but without the gendered language. This resulted in systematically undervaluing female candidates' qualifications, reinforcing gender biases instead of eliminating them.

Lack of Diversity Considerations

The recruitment tool's development process did not include mechanisms to detect and correct biases in the training data. Without these safeguards, the AI system could not differentiate between patterns that genuinely indicated job success and those that reflected the historical biases in the data.

By failing to account for diversity in its design, the AI system perpetuated discriminatory practices in hiring. Rather than serving as a neutral, objective tool for assessing candidates, the system became a vehicle for reinforcing existing inequalities. This disadvantaged female candidates and potentially overlooked highly qualified individuals whose profiles did not fit the historically male-dominated mould.

Deployment Without Ethical Review

The recruitment tool was tested internally at Amazon but did not undergo a thorough ethical review. Such a review could have flagged the bias issue by analysing the system's outputs and comparing them against a diverse set of resumes. An ethical review would have provided an opportunity to address these issues before the tool was used in hiring decisions.

The absence of an ethical review meant that the biases embedded in the tool went unnoticed until after it had already impacted hiring processes. This compromised the recruitment process's fairness and exposed Amazon to criticism and reputational risk. The failure to conduct an ethical review highlighted the dangers of deploying AI systems that have not been rigorously evaluated for fairness and bias, especially in areas that directly affect people's lives.

Lessons Learned

The development and subsequent failure of Amazon's AI recruitment tool provided valuable insights into the complexities of building fair and effective AI systems. The experience highlighted several critical areas where improvements are necessary to prevent similar issues in future projects.

Addressing these aspects is crucial to ensure that AI systems are technically sound and aligned with principles of fairness and inclusivity. By incorporating these lessons into the AI development process, organisations can create more equitable technologies that serve a broader range of users and help prevent the unintended consequences that can arise from biased or poorly tested systems.

The Critical Importance of Ensuring Diversity in Training Data

One key takeaway from Amazon's experience is ensuring that training data is diverse and representative of the broader population. This includes actively seeking and incorporating data from underrepresented groups to avoid perpetuating historical biases. For AI systems to be fair and effective, they must learn from a dataset that reflects the diversity of the people they will assess.

Regular audits of training data are also essential to identify and correct potential biases. This process should involve technical assessments and input from diversity experts to ensure the data used is as inclusive as possible.

The Necessity of Implementing Bias Detection and Mitigation Strategies:

AI systems, particularly those used in sensitive areas like recruitment, must include robust mechanisms for detecting and mitigating bias. These tools can help identify when AI produces biased outputs and allow developers to adjust the model accordingly. Techniques such as re-weighting, adversarial debiasing, and fairness constraints should be part of the AI development process to ensure that the system treats all candidates equitably.

Bias detection should not be a one-time process. Continuous monitoring is necessary to ensure the AI system remains fair over time, especially when encountering new data. This ongoing oversight helps prevent the reinforcement of biases and ensures that the system evolves in a way that promotes fairness.

The Value of Ethical AI Reviews and Audits

It must be stated how important it is to conduct thorough ethical reviews and audits before deploying AI systems. These reviews should assess the AI's technical performance and potential social and ethical impacts. Ethical audits provide a crucial checkpoint for identifying and addressing biases, ensuring that the AI operates consistently with the organisation's values and societal expectations.

Ethical reviews should involve diverse stakeholders, including ethicists, legal experts, and representatives from underrepresented groups. This cross-disciplinary approach helps ensure that the AI system is evaluated from multiple perspectives, increasing the likelihood that potential issues are identified and addressed before they can cause harm.

Conclusion

The failure of Amazon's AI recruitment tool underscores the critical importance of addressing bias and ethical considerations in AI development, particularly in sensitive applications like hiring. By learning from these mistakes, organisations can develop more fair, inclusive, and effective AI systems. This involves ensuring diversity in training data, implementing robust bias detection and mitigation strategies, and conducting thorough ethical reviews before deployment. These steps are essential for creating AI systems that perform technically well and uphold the principles of fairness and equity.

Google Photos - Image Recognition and Racial Bias

In 2015, Google faced significant backlash after its AI-powered image recognition software in Google Photos misidentified photos of black individuals as "gorillas." This incident revealed serious flaws in the underlying algorithms and exposed broader issues related to the lack of diversity in AI training datasets and inadequate testing procedures. The mistake served as a stark reminder of the potential for AI to perpetuate and even exacerbate societal biases when not carefully managed.

Failure Points

The Google Photos incident revealed significant flaws in the development and deployment of AI systems, particularly in the context of image recognition technology. The challenges faced by the AI model underscored the critical importance of inclusivity and thorough testing in designing AI systems that interact with diverse populations. These failures resulted in serious misclassifications and triggered widespread public backlash, highlighting the broader implications of biased AI in society. The issues surrounding Google Photos' image recognition software are a powerful example of the potential consequences when AI systems are not rigorously vetted for fairness and accuracy.

Training Data Inadequacy

Google Photos' AI model was trained on a dataset lacking sufficient diversity, particularly regarding skin tones and ethnic backgrounds. The model was primarily trained on images that overrepresented lighter-skinned individuals, which led to a significant gap in its ability to accurately identify and classify pictures of people with darker skin tones.

The training data did not adequately represent all demographics, so the AI struggled to generalise its image recognition capabilities across different racial groups. This lack of representation in the training data directly contributed to the egregious misclassification of black individuals as "gorillas," a deeply offensive and harmful error that highlighted the importance of inclusive datasets.

Inadequate Testing

Before its public release, Google Photos' image recognition software underwent testing. However, these tests were insufficiently rigorous to ensure the AI's accuracy across diverse demographic groups. The testing process did not include a comprehensive evaluation of the model's performance on images of people with darker skin tones, which allowed the bias to go undetected.

The lack of thorough testing across diverse populations was likely due to an overreliance on homogeneous data during the development and testing phases. Without deliberate efforts to include a wide range of demographic variables, the AI's biases were neither identified nor addressed, leading to public failure.

Public Outcry and Trust Issues

The misidentification of black individuals as "gorillas" triggered widespread public outrage, with many people expressing deep concern over the racial bias embedded in AI systems. The incident became a major public relations crisis for Google, casting doubt on the company's commitment to ethical AI development and raising broader questions about the potential harms of biased AI.

The incident damaged the public's trust in Google's AI capabilities, particularly in communities directly affected by the error. It highlighted the risks of deploying AI technologies that have not been adequately tested for fairness and accuracy, especially in sensitive areas like image recognition that directly impact people's lives and identities.

Lessons Learned

The challenges Google Photos' image recognition system faces underscore the importance of approaching AI development with a commitment to fairness, inclusivity, and ethical responsibility. When AI systems fail, especially in ways that impact marginalised groups, they cause immediate harm and erode public trust in technology. The lessons learned from such failures emphasise the need for deliberate and ongoing efforts to ensure that AI systems are trained, tested, and deployed in ways that reflect the diversity of the populations they serve. Moreover, transparency and accountability are crucial in addressing and rectifying issues, ensuring that AI technologies contribute positively to society.

The Need for Comprehensive and Diverse Training Datasets

One critical lesson from this incident is the importance of using comprehensive and diverse training datasets. AI systems must be trained on human diversity data, including skin tones, ethnicities, and cultural backgrounds. By ensuring that training datasets are inclusive, developers can reduce the risk of bias and improve the AI's ability to serve all user groups accurately.

Building diverse datasets is crucial, but updating and refining them is essential as new data becomes available continuously. This ongoing process helps AI systems adapt to changing societal norms and demographics, reducing the potential for biased outcomes.

Importance of Extensive Testing Across Different Demographic Groups

Before deployment, AI systems should undergo extensive testing across various demographic groups. This testing should include evaluating the model's performance on different skin tones, facial features, and other human diversity characteristics. Such testing is essential for identifying and eliminating biases that may not be apparent in more homogeneous testing environments.

Testing should also simulate real-world conditions as closely as possible, including the diversity of the user base that the AI will serve. This approach helps ensure the AI system performs well across all contexts and demographics, minimising the risk of bias-related failures.

The Necessity of Transparency and Accountability in AI Development

In the wake of such failures, companies must be transparent about what went wrong and what steps are taken to address the issues. Transparency builds trust with the public and demonstrates a commitment to ethical AI development. Companies should be open about their AI systems' limitations and proactively communicate how they plan to improve them.

Companies must take responsibility for the outcomes of their AI systems, including addressing any harm caused by biased or inaccurate models. This includes implementing ethical oversight processes involving diverse perspectives and stakeholders and ensuring AI development aligns with societal values and standards. Regular audits, ethical reviews, and public accountability mechanisms are essential for maintaining trust and ensuring that AI technologies are developed and deployed responsibly.

Conclusion

The Google Photos incident powerfully reminds us of the importance of diversity, thorough testing, and ethical accountability in AI development. By learning from these failures, companies can develop more inclusive, fair, and trustworthy AI systems that better serve all users. The incident underscores the need for a proactive approach to identifying and mitigating bias, ensuring that AI technologies contribute to a more equitable and just society.

References

- Amodei, D., Olah, C., Steinhardt, J., Christiano, P., Schulman, J., & Mané, D. (2016). Concrete Problems in AI Safety. arXiv preprint arXiv:1606.06565. DOI: https://doi.org/10.48550/arXiv.1606.06565
- Binns, R. (2018). Fairness in Machine Learning: Lessons from Political Philosophy. Proceedings of the 2018 Conference on Fairness, Accountability, and Transparency, 149-159. DOI:

- https://doi.org/10.1145/3287560.3287583
- Buolamwini, J., & Gebru, T. (2018). Gender Shades: Intersectional Accuracy Disparities in Commercial Gender Classification. Proceedings of the 1st Conference on Fairness, Accountability and Transparency, 77-91. DOI: https://doi.org/10.48550/arXiv.1801.04534
- Dastin, J. (2018). Amazon Scraps Secret AI Recruiting Tool That Showed Bias against Women. Reuters. Available at: https://www.reuters.com/article/us-amazon-com-jobs-automation-insight-idUSKCN1MK08G
- Mitchell, T. M., & Brynjolfsson, E. (2017). Track how technology is transforming work. Nature, 544(7650), 290-292. DOI: https://doi.org/10.1038/544290a
- Noble, S. U. (2018). Algorithms of Oppression: How Search Engines Reinforce Racism. NYU Press. ISBN: 978-1479837243
- O'Neil, C. (2016). Weapons of Math Destruction: How Big Data Increases Inequality and Threatens Democracy.

Crown Publishing Group. ISBN: 978-0553418811

Additional Reading Material

- Barocas, S., Hardt, M., & Narayanan, A. (2019). Fairness and Machine Learning. fairmlbook.org. ISBN: 978-1717416588
- Crawford, K., & Calo, R. (2016). There is a blind spot in AI research. Nature, 538(7625), 311-313. DOI: https://doi.org/10.1038/538311a
- Eubanks, V. (2018). Automating Inequality: How High-Tech Tools Profile, Police, and Punish the Poor. St. Martin's Press. ISBN: 978-1250074317
- Pasquale, F. (2015). The Black Box Society: The Secret Algorithms That Control Money and Information. Harvard University Press. ISBN: 978-0674970847
- Zuboff, S. (2019). The Age of Surveillance Capitalism: The Fight for a Human Future at the New Frontier of Power. PublicAffairs. ISBN: 978-1610395694

Appendices

Glossary of Key Terms

Algorithm	A set of rules or processes followed in problem-solving operations, often used by computers in data processing and automated reasoning.
Artificial Intelligence (AI)	The simulation of human intelligence in machines programmed to think like humans and mimic their actions.
Artificial Neural Networks (ANNs)	Computing systems inspired by the biological neural networks that constitute animal brains. These systems 'learn' to perform tasks by considering examples, generally without being programmed with task-specific rules.
Backpropagation	A supervised learning algorithm for training artificial neural networks, where the error is calculated and propagated back through the network to adjust the weights.

Bagging (Bootstrap Aggregating)	An ensemble technique that improves the accuracy and stability of machine learning algorithms by training multiple model versions on different subsets of data and averaging the results.
Binary Classification	A classification task that restricts the output to two possible classes, such as "spam" or "not spam."
Classification	A machine learning task of predicting a discrete label for an input, such as categorising an email as spam or not.
Clustering	A type of unsupervised learning where the task is to group a set of objects so that objects in the same group (called a cluster) are more similar than those in different groups.
Collaborative Filtering	A method recommender systems use to automatically predict a user's interests by collecting preferences from many users (collaborating).
Content-Based Filtering	A recommender system technique that uses features of an item and a user's profile to make recommendations.

Confusion Matrix	A table used to evaluate the performance of a classification algorithm, showing the actual versus predicted classifications.
Data Encoding	The process of converting categorical data into numerical format so that machine learning algorithms can process it.
Decision Tree	A decision support tool that uses a tree-like model of decisions and their possible consequences, including chance event outcomes, resource costs, and utility.
Deep Learning	A subset of machine learning in which artificial neural networks, algorithms inspired by the human brain, learn from large amounts of data.
Ensemble Learning	A machine learning paradigm where multiple models (often called "weak learners") are trained to solve the same problem and combined to get better results.
Generalisation	The ability of a machine learning model to adapt properly to new, previously unseen data drawn from the same distribution as the one used to create the model.

Gradient Boosting	A machine learning technique for regression and classification problems that produces a prediction model in the form of an ensemble of weak models, typically decision trees.
Hyperparameters	The parameters in machine learning algorithms that are set before the learning process begins and control the learning process.
K-Means Clustering	A type of unsupervised learning used when you have unlabelled data (i.e., data without defined categories or groups). The algorithm finds groups in the data, with the number of groups represented by the variable K.
Logistic Regression	A statistical method for predicting binary outcomes from data.
Machine Learning (ML)	A branch of artificial intelligence (AI) and computer science that uses data and algorithms to imitate how humans learn, gradually improving accuracy.
Neural Networks	A series of algorithms that attempt to recognise underlying relationships in a data set

	through a process miming how the human brain operates.
Overfitting	A modelling error in machine learning that occurs when a model is too closely fitted to a limited set of data points. This leads to poor predictive performance on new data.
Precision	A measure of the number of true positive predictions a model makes divided by the total number of positive predictions.
Recommender System	A subclass of information filtering systems that seeks to predict a user's preference or rating for an item.
Regression	A predictive modelling technique that estimates the relationships among variables. It is often used to forecast outcomes and make predictions based on historical data.
Reinforcement Learning (RL)	A type of machine learning where an agent learns to behave in an environment by performing actions and seeing the results.
Stacking	An ensemble learning technique that combines multiple classification or regression

	models via a meta-classifier or meta-regressor.
Support Vector Machines (SVMs)	A set of supervised learning methods for detecting classification, regression, and outliers.
Supervised Learning	A type of machine learning where the algorithm is trained on a labelled dataset, which means that each training example is paired with an output label.
Unsupervised Learning	A type of machine learning that looks for previously undetected patterns in a dataset with no pre-existing labels and with a minimum of human supervision.
Validation	The process of evaluating the performance of a model on a validation set during training to tune the model's hyperparameters and prevent overfitting.
Variance	The degree to which a model's predictions differ across different data points. High variance can lead to overfitting.

List of Figures

FIGURE 1: DIFFERENCE BETWEEN CONVENTIONAL PROGRAMMING AND PROGRAMMING FOR MACHINE LEARNING. 3
FIGURE 2: EXAMPLE OF LABEL ENCODING. 24
FIGURE 3: EXAMPLE OF ONE-HOT ENCODING. 25
FIGURE 4: EXAMPLE OF CONFUSION MATRIX. 27
FIGURE 5: EXAMPLE OF LINEAR AND POLYNOMIAL REGRESSION. 39
FIGURE 6: EXAMPLE OF A SCATTER PLOT BETWEEN TWO PARAMETERS. ... 66
FIGURE 7: THE FARMER'S MARKETS IN THE USA ARE DIVIDED INTO THREE CLUSTERS. 68
FIGURE 8: EXAMPLE OF FOUR CLUSTERS CREATED USING THE K-MEANS ALGORITHM. 69
FIGURE 9: DETERMINING THE REQUIRED NUMBER OF CLUSTERS USING THE ELBOW METHOD. 71
FIGURE 10: A DENDROGRAM SHOWING HIERARCHICAL CLUSTERS. (SOURCE: GOOGLE IMAGES) 73
FIGURE 11: EXAMPLE OUTPUT OF DBSCAN. (SOURCE: GOOGLE IMAGES) 78
FIGURE 12: SCHEMATIC DIAGRAM OF AN ARTIFICIAL NEURON (A PERCEPTRON). Σ IS THE SUMMATION FUNCTION, AND Z IS THE ACTIVATION FUNCTION. 87
FIGURE 13: A MULTI-LAYER PERCEPTRON (MLP) TO SOLVE THE XOR PROBLEM. 88
FIGURE 14: A DEEP NEURAL NETWORK FOR DETECTING HANDWRITTEN DIGITS USING THE MNIST DATASET. 90
FIGURE 15: LSTM ARCHITECTURE. 95
FIGURE 16: GRU ARCHITECTURE. 96

Suggested Resources for Further Reference

Books

Aggarwal, C. C. (2016). Recommender Systems: The Textbook. Springer. ISBN: 978-3-319-29658-0

Amatriain, X., & Basilico, J. (2012). Netflix Recommendations: Beyond the 5 stars (Part 1). https://netflixtechblog.com/netflix-recommendations-beyond-the-5-stars-part-1-55838468f429

Amodei, D., Olah, C., Steinhardt, J., Christiano, P., Schulman, J., & Mané, D. (2016). Concrete Problems in AI Safety. arXiv preprint arXiv:1606.06565. DOI: https://doi.org/10.48550/arXiv.1606.06565

Barocas, S., Hardt, M., & Narayanan, A. (2019). Fairness and Machine Learning. fairmlbook.org. ISBN: 978-1717416588

Binns, R. (2018). Fairness in Machine Learning: Lessons from Political Philosophy. Proceedings of the 2018 Conference on Fairness, Accountability, and Transparency, 149-159. DOI: https://doi.org/10.1145/3287560.3287583

Bird, S., Klein, E., & Loper, E. (2009). Natural Language Processing with Python. ISBN: 978-0596516499

Bishop, C. M. (2006). Pattern Recognition and Machine Learning. Springer. ISBN: 978-0387310732

Box, G. E. P., Jenkins, G. M., & Reinsel, G. C. (2015). Time Series Analysis: Forecasting and Control (5th ed.). Wiley. ISBN: 978-1118675021

Breiman, L. (2001). Random forests. Machine Learning, 45(1), 5-32. DOI: https://doi.org/10.1023/A:1010933404324

Brockman, G., Cheung, V., Pettersson, L., Schneider, J., Schulman, J., Tang, J., & Zaremba, W. (2016). OpenAI Gym. arXiv preprint arXiv:1606.01540. DOI: https://doi.org/10.48550/arXiv.1606.01540

Brown, T. B., Mann, B., Ryder, N., Subbiah, M., Kaplan, J., Dhariwal, P., ... & Amodei, D. (2020). Language Models are Few-Shot Learners. Advances in Neural Information Processing Systems, 33, 1877-1901. DOI: https://doi.org/10.48550/arXiv.2005.14165

Buolamwini, J., & Gebru, T. (2018). Gender Shades: Intersectional Accuracy Disparities in Commercial Gender Classification. Proceedings of the 1st Conference on Fairness, Accountability and Transparency, 77-91. DOI: https://doi.org/10.48550/arXiv.1801.04534

Burke, R., Mobasher, B., & Zhang, J. (2013). Privacy-Preserving Recommender Systems: Challenges and Opportunities. ACM Transactions on Internet Technology (TOIT), 13(1), 1-26. DOI: https://doi.org/10.1145/2542182.2542191

Chatfield, C. (2003). The Analysis of Time Series: An Introduction (6th ed.). CRC Press. ISBN: 978-1584883173

Chen, L., Mislove, A., & Wilson, C. (2015). Peeking Beneath the Hood of Uber. In Proceedings of the 2015 ACM Conference on Internet Measurement Conference (pp. 495-508). DOI: https://doi.org/10.1145/2815675.2815681

Chollet, F. (2018). Deep Learning with Python. Manning Publications. ISBN: 978-1617294433

Cosley, D., Lam, S. K., Albert, I., Konstan, J. A., & Riedl, J. (2003). Is seeing believing? How recommender system interfaces affect users' opinions. Proceedings of the SIGCHI Conference on Human Factors in Computing Systems. DOI: https://doi.org/10.1145/642611.642713

Crawford, K., & Calo, R. (2016). There is a blind spot in AI research. Nature, 538(7625), 311-313. DOI: https://doi.org/10.1038/538311a

Dastin, J. (2018). Amazon Scraps Secret AI Recruiting Tool That Showed Bias against Women. Reuters. Available at: https://www.reuters.com/article/us-amazon-com-jobs-automation-insight-idUSKCN1MK08G

Daugherty, P. R., & Wilson, H. J. (2018). Human + Machine: Reimagining Work in the Age of AI. Harvard Business Review Press. ISBN: 978-1633693869

Dean, J., & Corrado, G. (2015). Large Scale Deep Learning for Intelligent Computer Systems. Communications of the ACM, 58(4), 56-65. DOI: https://doi.org/10.1145/2699415

Diebold, F. X. (2012). Elements of Forecasting (4th ed.). Cengage Learning. ISBN: 978-0324359047

Dietterich, T. G. (2000). Ensemble methods in machine learning. International Workshop on Multiple Classifier Systems, 1-15. Springer. DOI: https://doi.org/10.1007/3-540-45014-9_1

Domingos, P. (2015). The Master Algorithm: How the Quest for the Ultimate Learning Machine Will Remake Our World. Basic Books. ISBN: 978-0465065707

Draper, N. R., & Smith, H. (1998). Applied Regression Analysis (3rd ed.). Wiley. ISBN: 978-0471170822

Ester, M., Kriegel, H.-P., Sander, J., & Xu, X. (1996). A Density-Based Algorithm for Discovering Clusters in Large Spatial Databases with Noise. Proceedings of the Second International Conference on Knowledge Discovery and Data Mining, 226-231. ISBN: 1-57735-004-9

Eubanks, V. (2018). Automating Inequality: How High-Tech Tools Profile, Police, and Punish the Poor. St. Martin's Press. ISBN: 978-1250074317

Fox, J. (2015). Applied Regression Analysis and Generalized Linear Models (3rd ed.). SAGE Publications, Inc. ISBN: 978-1452205663

Francois-Lavet, V., Henderson, P., Islam, R., Bellemare, M. G., & Pineau, J. (2018). An introduction to deep reinforcement learning. Foundations and Trends in Machine Learning, 11(3-4), 219-354. DOI: https://doi.org/10.1561/2200000071

Freund, Y., & Schapire, R. E. (1997). A decision-theoretic generalization of on-line learning and an application to boosting. Journal of Computer and System Sciences, 55(1), 119-139. DOI: https://doi.org/10.1006/jcss.1997.1504

Friedman, J. H. (2001). Greedy function approximation: A gradient boosting machine. Annals of Statistics, 29(5), 1189-1232. DOI: https://doi.org/10.1214/aos/1013203451

Gelman, A., & Hill, J. (2006). Data Analysis Using Regression and Multilevel/Hierarchical Models. Cambridge University Press. ISBN: 978-0521686891

Géron, A. (2019). Hands-On Machine Learning with Scikit-Learn, Keras, and TensorFlow (2nd ed.). O'Reilly Media. ISBN: 978-1492032649

Goldberg, Y. (2017). Neural Network Methods for Natural Language Processing. ISBN: 978-1627052986

Goodfellow, I., Bengio, Y., & Courville, A. (2016). Deep Learning. MIT Press. ISBN: 978-0262035613

Hamilton, J. D. (1994). Time Series Analysis. Princeton University Press. ISBN: 978-0691042893

Hastie, T., Tibshirani, R., & Friedman, J. (2009). The Elements of Statistical Learning: Data Mining, Inference, and Prediction (2nd ed.). Springer. ISBN: 978-0387848570

Hochreiter, S., & Schmidhuber, J. (1997). Long short-term memory. Neural Computation, 9(8), 1735-1780. DOI: https://doi.org/10.1162/neco.1997.9.8.1735

Holt, C. C. (2004). Forecasting seasonals and trends by exponentially weighted moving averages. International Journal of Forecasting, 20(1), 5-10. DOI: https://doi.org/10.1016/j.ijforecast.2003.09.015

Hyndman, R. J., & Athanasopoulos, G. (2018). Forecasting: Principles and Practice (2nd ed.). OTexts. ISBN: 978-0987507112

James, G., Witten, D., Hastie, T., & Tibshirani, R. (2013). An Introduction to Statistical Learning: with Applications in R. Springer. ISBN: 978-1461471370

Jannach, D., Zanker, M., & Felfering, A. (2010). Recommender Systems: An Introduction. Cambridge University Press. ISBN: 978-0-521-49336-9

Jordan, M. I., & Mitchell, T. M. (2015). Machine learning: Trends, perspectives, and prospects. Science, 349(6245), 255-260. DOI: https://doi.org/10.1126/science.aaa8415

Jurafsky, D., & Martin, J. H. (2008). Speech and Language Processing. ISBN: 978-0131873216

Koller, D., & Friedman, N. (2009). Probabilistic Graphical Models: Principles and Techniques. MIT Press. ISBN: 978-0262013192

Koren, Y., Bell, R., & Volinsky, C. (2009). Matrix Factorization Techniques for Recommender Systems. IEEE Computer, 42(8), 30-37. DOI: https://doi.org/10.1109/MC.2009.263

Krizhevsky, A., Sutskever, I., & Hinton, G. E. (2012). ImageNet classification with deep convolutional neural networks. Advances in Neural Information Processing Systems, 25, 1097-1105. DOI: https://doi.org/10.1145/3065386

Kuhn, M., & Johnson, K. (2013). Applied Predictive Modeling. Springer. ISBN: 978-1461468486

Kuncheva, L. I. (2004). Combining Pattern Classifiers: Methods and Algorithms. Wiley-Interscience. ISBN: 978-0471210788

Kutner, M. H., Nachtsheim, C. J., & Neter, J. (2004). Applied Linear Regression Models (4th ed.). McGraw-Hill/Irwin. ISBN: 978-0073014661

LeCun, Y., Bengio, Y., & Hinton, G. (2015). Deep learning. Nature, 521(7553), 436-444. DOI: https://doi.org/10.1038/nature14539

Li, Y. (2017). Deep reinforcement learning: An overview. arXiv preprint arXiv:1701.07274. DOI: https://doi,org/10.48550/arXiv.1701.07274

Lillicrap, T. P., Hunt, J. J., Pritzel, A., Heess, N., Erez, T., Tassa, Y., ... & Wierstra, D. (2016). Continuous control with deep reinforcement learning. arXiv preprint arXiv:1509.02971. DOI: https://doi.org/10.48550/arXiv.1509.02971

Liu, B. (2012). Sentiment Analysis and Opinion Mining. ISBN: 978-1608458844

Makridakis, S., Wheelwright, S. C., & Hyndman, R. J. (1998). Forecasting: Methods and Applications (3rd ed.). Wiley. ISBN: 978-0471532330

Manning, C. D., Raghavan, P., & Schütze, H. (2008). Introduction to Information Retrieval. ISBN: 978-0521865715

Meir, R., & Rätsch, G. (2003). An introduction to boosting and leveraging. In Advanced Lectures on Machine Learning, 119-184. Springer. DOI: https://doi.org/10.1007/978-3-540-28650-9_4

Mitchell, M. (2019). Artificial Intelligence: A Guide for Thinking Humans. Penguin. ISBN: 978-0241404829

Mitchell, T. M. (1997). Machine Learning. McGraw-Hill. ISBN: 978-0070428072

Mitchell, T. M., & Brynjolfsson, E. (2017). Track how technology is transforming work. Nature, 544(7650), 290-292. DOI: https://doi.org/10.1038/544290a

Mnih, V., Kavukcuoglu, K., Silver, D., Rusu, A. A., Veness, J., Bellemare, M. G., ... & Hassabis, D. (2015). Human-level control through deep reinforcement learning. Nature,

518(7540), 529-533. DOI: https://doi.org/10.1038/nature14236

Montgomery, D. C., Peck, E. A., & Vining, G. G. (2012). Introduction to Linear Regression Analysis (5th ed.). Wiley. ISBN: 978-0470542811

Murphy, K. P. (2012). Machine Learning: A Probabilistic Perspective. MIT Press. ISBN: 978-0262018029

Noble, S. U. (2018). Algorithms of Oppression: How Search Engines Reinforce Racism. NYU Press. ISBN: 978-1479837243

O'Neil, C. (2016). Weapons of Math Destruction: How Big Data Increases Inequality and Threatens Democracy. Crown Publishing Group. ISBN: 978-0553418811

Pasquale, F. (2015). The Black Box Society: The Secret Algorithms That Control Money and Information. Harvard University Press. ISBN: 978-0674970847

Pedregosa, F., Varoquaux, G., Gramfort, A., Michel, V., Thirion, B., Grisel, O., ... & Duchesnay, E. (2011). Scikit-learn: Machine Learning in Python. Journal of Machine Learning Research, 12, 2825-2830. Available at: https://jmlr.csail.mit.edu/papers/volume12/pedregosa11a/pedregosa11a.pdf

Pinker, S. (1994). The Language Instinct. ISBN: 978-0060976514

Polikar, R. (2006). Ensemble based systems in decision making. IEEE Circuits and Systems Magazine, 6(3), 21-45. DOI: https://doi.org/10.1109/MCAS.2006.1688199

Puterman, M. L. (2014). Markov Decision Processes: Discrete Stochastic Dynamic Programming. John Wiley & Sons. ISBN: 9781118625873

Ricci, F., Rokach, L., & Shapira, B. (2015). Recommender Systems Handbook. Springer. ISBN: 978-1-4899-7637-6

Rumelhart, D. E., Hinton, G. E., & Williams, R. J. (1986). Learning representations by back-propagating errors. Nature, 323(6088), 533-536. DOI: https://doi.org/10.1038/323533a0

Russell, S., & Norvig, P. (2010). Artificial Intelligence: A Modern Approach. ISBN: 978-0136042594

Schafer, J. B., Konstan, J. A., & Riedl, J. (2001). E-commerce recommendation applications. Data Mining and Knowledge Discovery, 5(1-2), 115-153. DOI: https://doi.org/10.1023/A:1009804230409

Scikit-learn Documentation. Available at: https://scikit-learn.org/stable/documentation.html

Seber, G. A. F., & Lee, A. J. (2012). Linear Regression Analysis (2nd ed.). Wiley. ISBN: 978-0471415404

Shumway, R. H., & Stoffer, D. S. (2017). Time Series Analysis and Its Applications: With R Examples (4th ed.). Springer. ISBN: 978-3319524511

Silver, D., Huang, A., Maddison, C. J., Guez, A., Sifre, L., Van Den Driessche, G., ... & Hassabis, D. (2016). Mastering the game of Go with deep neural networks and tree search. Nature, 529(7587), 484-489. DOI: https://doi.org/10.1038/nature16961

Sutton, R. S., & Barto, A. G. (2018). Reinforcement Learning: An Introduction (2nd ed.). MIT Press. ISBN: 978-0262039246

Tan, P.-N., Steinbach, M., & Kumar, V. (2006). Introduction to Data Mining. Pearson Education. ISBN: 978-0321321367

Tomsett, R., & Preece, A. (2019). Watson for Genomics: Machine Learning for Precision Medicine. IBM Journal of Research and Development, 63(6), 1-7. DOI: https://doi.org/10.1147/JRD.2019.2952073

Topol, E. (2019). High-performance medicine: the convergence of human and artificial intelligence. Nature Medicine, 25, 44-56. DOI: https://doi.org/10.1038/s41591-018-0300-7

Tsay, R. S. (2010). Analysis of Financial Time Series (3rd ed.). Wiley. ISBN: 978-0470414354

Vaswani, A., Shazeer, N., Parmar, N., Uszkoreit, J., Jones, L., Gomez, A. N., ... & Polosukhin, I. (2017). Attention is all you need. Advances in Neural Information Processing Systems, 30, 5998-6008. DOI: https://doi.org/10.48550/arXiv.1706.03762

Weisberg, S. (2014). Applied Linear Regression (4th ed.). Wiley. ISBN: 978-1118386088

Witten, I. H., & Frank, E. (2016). Data Mining: Practical Machine Learning Tools and Techniques. Morgan Kaufmann. ISBN: 978-0128042915

Wolpert, D. H. (1992). Stacked generalization. Neural Networks, 5(2), 241-259. DOI: https://doi.org/10.1016/S0893-6080(05)80023-1

Wooldridge, J. M. (2015). Introductory Econometrics: A Modern Approach (6th ed.). Cengage Learning. ISBN: 978-1305270107

Zhou, Z.-H. (2012). Ensemble Methods: Foundations and Algorithms. CRC Press. ISBN: 978-1439830031

Zuboff, S. (2019). The Age of Surveillance Capitalism: The Fight for a Human Future at the New Frontier of Power. PublicAffairs. ISBN: 978-1610395694

Websites

KDnuggets - (https://www.kdnuggets.com) - A leading site on data science, machine learning, and AI, offering tutorials, news, and resources.

Towards Data Science (TDS) - (https://towardsdatascience.com) - A popular platform with articles on machine learning, AI, and data science written by practitioners and researchers.

Machine Learning Mastery - (https://www.machinelearningmastery.com) - Focuses on practical, hands-on machine learning and deep learning tutorials.

ArXiv - (https://arxiv.org) - A free distribution service and an open-access archive for scholarly articles in physics, mathematics, computer science, quantitative biology, quantitative finance, and statistics, with many papers on machine learning.

Scikit-learn Documentation - (https://scikit-learn.org/stable/documentation.html) - Official documentation for Scikit-learn, a key library in Python for machine learning.

Journals

Journal of Machine Learning Research (JMLR) - A leading journal focusing on research in machine learning. Accessible at http://www.jmlr.org.

IEEE Transactions on Neural Networks and Learning Systems - Publishes high-quality technical papers on neural networks and learning systems. Available through IEEE Xplore.

Nature Machine Intelligence - Covers a broad range of AI and machine learning topics, including research articles, reviews, and opinion pieces.

Pattern Recognition - A journal that publishes articles on all aspects of pattern recognition, including machine learning methods.

Machine Learning - A journal that publishes scientific articles on machine learning.

Online Courses

Coursera - Machine Learning by Stanford University - A foundational course taught by Andrew Ng, available at https://www.coursera.org/learn/machine-learning.

edX - Data Science and Machine Learning Essentials by Microsoft - An introductory course on machine learning as part of the Microsoft Professional Program, accessible via https://www.edx.org/course/data-science-essentials.

Udacity - Deep Learning Nanodegree - Focuses on deep learning, covering neural networks, convolutional networks, and more. Available on https://www.udacity.com/course/deep-learning-nanodegree--nd101.

Fast.ai - Practical Deep Learning for Coders - A free course offering practical deep-learning tutorials, accessible at https://www.fast.ai.

Harvard Online - Data Science: Machine Learning - Part of the Harvard Data Science Professional Certificate program, available at https://online-learning.harvard.edu/course/data-science-machine-learning.

About the Author

Partha Majumdar's leadership in the dynamic realm of software solutions is about technical prowess, strategic insight, and a unique style that blends these qualities with a personal touch. This makes his approach to innovation, efficiency, and business success unique.

His educational journey, which spans a Global Doctor of Business Administration to specialisations in Computational Data Sciences and Cybersecurity, reflects a commitment to continuous learning.

Majumdar's professional journey has been nothing short of extraordinary. As the Vice President of Software Engineering at J.P. Morgan Chase and Co. in his last role, he has spearheaded impactful initiatives, contributing to the evolution of software development paradigms. He is in the inception phase of starting his firm in the UAE and pursuing his PhD in Computer Science from Kalinga University. His earlier role as the Managing Director of Majumdar Consultancy Private Limited showcased his entrepreneurial spirit, where he successfully nurtured a fledgling business into a success with a global footprint.

Partha Majumdar's diverse talents and expertise are not confined to a single domain. His proficiency in software development, predictive modelling, descriptive data analysis, and Agile Project Management is a testament to his versatility, adaptability, and ability to deliver innovative solutions across various contexts.

Beyond his roles in corporate leadership, Majumdar has been recognised with numerous awards, including the "Excellence Award," "Gratitude Award," "Merit Award," and "Best IT Manager," underscoring his impact and leadership in the field. His commitment to excellence is further demonstrated through a comprehensive list of professional upskilling, covering project management, IT service management, and specialised areas like data science and cloud computing.

Majumdar's publications and patent attempts showcase a commitment to advancing the field. He has published twenty-one books on academia and knowledge dissemination, and his upcoming books and publications illustrate his dedication to sharing knowledge and insights.

In conclusion, Partha Majumdar's career is a testament to his multifaceted expertise, from spearheading successful ventures to influencing software development paradigms at industry giants. His unwavering commitment to innovation, coupled with a rich educational background and many certificates, positions him as a distinguished leader poised to continue making impactful contributions in the ever-evolving landscape of software solutions.

Books by the Author

Mastering Classification Algorithms for Machine Learning

This book delves into the core of machine learning through the lens of classification algorithms, which play a pivotal role in categorising input based on its features. These algorithms are the backbone of various applications, from spam detection to fraud prevention. Starting with a foundational overview of problem-solving in machine learning, the book transitions to a focused examination of classification challenges. It provides an in-depth exploration of the Naïve Bayes algorithm, Logistic Regression, including the crucial sigmoid function, and Decision Trees, highlighting critical concepts like the Gini Factor and Entropy. Furthermore, it elaborates on the Random Forest algorithm and concludes with an insightful discussion on Boosting techniques, offering a comprehensive guide to mastering classification algorithms in machine learning.

Link in Amazon Store:
https://www.amazon.com/dp/935551851X

Machine Learning for Managers

This book is a comprehensive guide tailored for leaders aiming to leverage machine learning (ML) within their organisations. It simplifies ML concepts, emphasising strategic applications over technical complexity. The book covers integrating ML into business practices, ethical data use, and real-world industry applications, showcasing ML's role in enhancing operations and innovation. It also provides insights on team building in the ML era, promoting cross-disciplinary collaboration for effective ML adoption. This book is a strategic roadmap for managers to harness ML, driving informed decision-making and positioning their organisations for future success in an AI-driven landscape.

Link in Amazon Store: https://www.amazon.in/dp/B0CZ5XTQ1L

Deep Learning for Managers

This book is a pivotal guide for modern leaders navigating the AI revolution. It demystifies deep learning, making it accessible to managers without requiring deep technical knowledge. This book equips leaders with the insights to harness AI effectively, covering everything from the basics of artificial neural networks to the ethical considerations of AI deployment. It's an indispensable resource for any leader aiming to leverage deep learning as a strategic asset in today's rapidly evolving business landscape.

Link in Amazon Store: https://www.amazon.in/dp/B0CWDPWSN8

Generative AI for Managers

This book is a cutting-edge guide that demystifies Generative AI for business leaders eager to harness this technology for growth and innovation. It delves into how Generative AI can revolutionise aspects of business, from enhancing customer experiences to optimising operations and driving strategic decision-making. The book provides a wealth of practical applications, showcases how mundane tasks can be automated for efficiency, and presents strategies for fostering a culture of innovation through AI. Additionally, it offers guidance on the ethical implementation of AI technologies, ensuring they complement and augment human capabilities within the organisational framework, thereby paving the way for a future rich in opportunities and advancements.

Link in Amazon Store: https://www.amazon.in/dp/B0CXYBFJHD

ChatGPT AI for Managers

This book is a vital resource for leaders navigating the AI revolution, focusing on integrating Generative AI, like ChatGPT, in enhancing managerial functions and team dynamics. It provides practical insights into leveraging ChatGPT to streamline tasks, bolster decision-making, and encourage innovative thinking within teams. This guide transcends theoretical knowledge, offering actionable strategies for managers to complement their skills with AI, thereby elevating their leadership effectiveness. Through real-world applications and expert advice, readers will learn to harmonise traditional management with AI advancements, ensuring they remain at the forefront of the evolving business environment.

Link in Amazon Store: https://www.amazon.in/dp/B0CY8L4CQ9

Data Lakes for Managers

This book is a guide tailored for managers, detailing how to utilise data lakes effectively. It simplifies complex concepts and focuses on practical strategies and the strategic use of data lake technologies like AWS, Azure, and GCP. The book addresses common challenges such as data silos and security. It offers insights into the future of data technologies, empowering managers to harness data for strategic decision-making and innovation.

Link in Amazon Store: https://www.amazon.in/dp/B0D35RCDPD

Recommendation Systems for Managers

This book demystifies the complexities of data-driven recommendation systems in an easy-to-understand format tailored for managers. This insightful guide traverses Time Series and Market Basket Analysis, AI, ML, and emerging technologies, offering a practical roadmap for implementing these systems. It's an indispensable resource for managers aiming to harness recommendation systems for strategic business decisions in the digital age.

Link in Amazon Store: https://www.amazon.in/dp/B0CXNNSJRC

Learn Emotion Analysis with R

This book is a comprehensive guide to Emotion Analysis using Lexicons, offering a step-by-step code walkthrough for developing Sentiment and Emotion Analysis systems with data from WhatsApp and Twitter. It introduces R and Shiny programming, which is essential for building emotion analysis systems. The discussion then extends to the fundamentals of Sentiment and Emotion Analysis, leading to the creation of Shiny applications tailored for this purpose. The book concludes by developing a specialised tool for analysing emotions from Twitter and WhatsApp data. Additionally, it hints at advancing into Machine Learning for Emotion Analysis, contingent on the availability of labelled data, positioning this as a subsequent step for readers.

Link in Amazon Store: https://www.amazon.com/dp/B096K2SVF2

Starting a New AI Business

This book is a comprehensive guide designed for entrepreneurs looking to harness the power of artificial intelligence to build successful enterprises. Covering everything from defining business purpose and understanding AI fundamentals to exploring innovative business models and identifying market opportunities, this book provides practical insights and strategic guidance. With case studies of industry giants and lessons from ancient wisdom, it equips readers with the tools and knowledge to navigate the AI landscape effectively and achieve sustainable growth.

Link in Amazon Store: https://www.amazon.in/dp/B0CL3YBSF8

Ten Essays on AI

This book offers a deep dive into the world of artificial intelligence, covering critical topics such as data-analytic thinking, data quality, AI strategies, and the evolution of AI technology. This comprehensive collection provides readers with practical insights and theoretical knowledge to harness AI's potential and navigate its challenges effectively.

Link in Amazon Store: https://www.amazon.in/dp/B0D9PMJBWB

Linear Programming for Project Management Professionals

This guide provides project management professionals with strategies for project crashing using linear programming, ensuring timely completion and cost efficiency. It introduces basic project management concepts, monitoring techniques, and linear programming problem formulation. The book explains how to solve these problems using Microsoft Excel's Solver and applying time and cost optimisation methods to real-world scenarios. It equips project management teams with a comprehensive toolkit to handle complex challenges effectively.

Link in Amazon Store: https://www.amazon.com/dp/B09PD1GFMY

Gartner Research Analysis

The book provides a clear framework for leveraging insights from the Gartner Hype-Cycle Report, an essential resource for understanding technological trends. It simplifies identifying and evaluating emerging technologies, their developers, and market readiness. A live case study illustrates practical application while emphasising the need for comprehensive research beyond the report. Essential for those seeking strategic technological guidance, this book demystifies the complex data presented in the Gartner Hype Cycle.

Link in Amazon Store: https://www.amazon.com/dp/B0CK582Y2M

Corporate Lessons I Learned

This book encapsulates 34 years of corporate experiences up to 2023, presenting a collection of impactful incidents and interactions that shaped the author's career. Primarily aimed at middle and lower-level managers, it offers humorous and insightful recollections that serve as practical guidelines for navigating daily challenges in the corporate world. The author illustrates valuable lessons learned through various encounters, making it a helpful resource for understanding and excelling in corporate management.

Link in Amazon Store: https://www.amazon.in/dp/B0CL3YBSF8

Mutual Fund Investing

This book is a comprehensive guide for middle-class investors in India, simplifying mutual funds. It covers types of mutual funds, differences between open-ended and closed funds, systematic investments, tax implications, and risk assessment. It also teaches advanced techniques like Piotrowski's F-Score and Mohanram's G-Score for building diversified portfolios and evaluating fund performance. Suitable for beginners and seasoned investors, it is essential for achieving financial growth and security through mutual funds.

Link in Amazon Store: https://www.amazon.com/dp/B0CYNG6B12

Creating an Investment Portfolio

This book delves into the scientific process of making informed investment decisions, highlighting the importance for individuals and corporations. It explores critical theories and applications in portfolio creation, covering various investment vehicles like fixed deposits, mutual funds, and shares, emphasising the necessary mathematics. Additionally, it introduces simple yet widely used tools for investment calculations. Designed to be accessible to a broad audience, this book is an invaluable guide for beginners and experienced investors aiming to enhance their understanding and effectiveness in investing.

Link in Amazon Store: https://www.amazon.com/dp/B0CK99SPKZ

Essay on the Indian Knowledge System – Part 1

The book delves into the Indian Knowledge System (IKS), a comprehensive approach to compiling, conserving, and disseminating India's rich knowledge heritage across various disciplines such as science, mathematics, social sciences, medicine, philosophy, art, and spirituality. It highlights the global perspective of IKS and its relevance in sharing India's intellectual legacy with the world. The study of Indology, or "Bharatatattva," as it's known in Indian scholarship, further explores the historical, cultural, linguistic, and literary facets of the Indian subcontinent. Through a series of concise essays, this book, one of a trilogy on ancient India, offers insights into Bharatatattva, underscoring India's significant contributions to global knowledge.

Link in Amazon Store: https://www.amazon.com/dp/B0CXNN95TR

Good People Are Tested the Most

This book explores the lives of seven extraordinary individuals who faced immense challenges and emerged victorious. The book delves into resilience, faith, and the triumph of the human spirit, featuring Bhakt Prahalad, Raja Harishchandra, Lord Shri Ram, Arjun, Hercules, Swami Vivekananda, and Sardar Milkha Singh. Their inspiring stories highlight the importance of maintaining principles, overcoming significant challenges, and the ultimate triumph of good over evil, serving as inspiration for all.

Link in Amazon Store: https://www.amazon.in/dp/B0D1FM44H9

Sailing through the Kali Yug

This book explores the relevance of ancient Indian scriptures, especially the Purans, in understanding the complexities of the present age. It introduces the concept of Yugs, highlighting Rishi Krishna Dwaipayan Ved Vyas's role and the Purans' structure. The book details the moral decline of the Kali Yug, starting from Raja Parikshit's reign, and emphasises Dharam's four pillars. It promotes Bhakti and practical spiritual practices as pathways to maintaining integrity and achieving liberation.

Link in Amazon Store:
https://www.amazon.in/dp/B0D6M34JCT

The Maha Purans in Brief

This book distils the essence of eighteen ancient Vedic scriptures, offering insights into their themes, stories, and teachings. The book explores the relevance of Puranic wisdom in modern life, providing guidance on ethics, leadership, environmental sustainability, and personal development. It serves as an accessible guide to understanding the rich spiritual heritage of Indian culture and applying its timeless lessons to contemporary challenges.

Link in Amazon Store:
https://www.amazon.in/dp/B0CW8GJ22L

Weekend in Jordan

Thanks to the country's visa-on-arrival policy for Indians, the authors spontaneously travelled to Jordan to celebrate their 20th wedding anniversary. Their weekend was filled with memorable experiences, from Petra's historical wonders to the Dead Sea's unique allure and Amman's vibrant city life. Despite its modest size, Jordan's rich offerings left a lasting impression. This book recounts their remarkable journey, providing insights into the treasures of Jordan.

Link in Amazon Store:
https://www.amazon.com/dp/B0CK5N6B3W

Elephant Ride in Chang Wangpo

In 2022, Thailand saw a significant influx of approximately 11.5 million tourists, underlining tourism's vital role in its economy, contributing around 6% to the Thai GDP. Reflecting on their past residency in Bangkok from 1996 to 1999, the authors seized a chance to revisit Thailand in 2018, noticing considerable changes. An efficient metro system has alleviated the once notorious Bangkok traffic, enhancing city navigation. While many cherished aspects remained, improvements in the road network and increased attractions enriched their experience. Coinciding with their 26th wedding anniversary, the business trip also included leisure exploration in Bangkok and Kanchanaburi, with a memorable visit to Chang Wangpo, blending nostalgia, discovery, and celebration.

Link in Amazon Store: https://www.amazon.com/dp/B0CKGWH97S

Weekend in South Sikkim

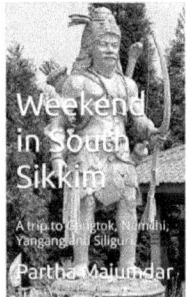

This book explores the less-travelled South Sikkim, diverging from popular tourist spots like Gangtok and Nathu La Pass. It covers captivating destinations such as Tsomgo Lake, Baba Ka Mandir, and Temi Tea Gardens. The authors delve into the cultural and spiritual essence of South Sikkim with visits to Namchi's Char Dham and Samdruptse Monastery. The narrative also extends to Yangang and the Bengal Safari in Siliguri, West Bengal, offering a comprehensive travelogue with diverse experiences.

Link in Amazon Store:
https://www.amazon.com/dp/B0CKL1DNTJ

Trips to Dubai

This travelogue unveils the multifaceted allure of Dubai, a top-tier tourist hub known for landmarks like the Burj Khalifa and Burj Al Arab, alongside thrilling experiences such as helicopter rides and dolphin encounters at the Atlantis. It extends beyond Dubai, shedding light on Abu Dhabi and Sharjah attractions, like the adrenaline-pumping Ferrari World and the enchanting Desert Safari. The author shares personal adventures, offering insights into the intricacies of visiting Dubai and navigating the Gulf region, making this book a valuable resource for anyone looking to explore the rich experiences Dubai and its neighbouring emirates offer.

Link in Amazon Store: https://www.amazon.com/dp/B0CKRYQKDN

1-Day Trips from Bengaluru

From 1975 to 2023, Bengaluru evolved from a retirees' haven to India's Silicon Valley, also renowned as Garden City. While Bengaluru has numerous tourist attractions and activity hubs, the city's vicinity offers many exploration destinations. This book focuses on day-trip-worthy spots around Bengaluru, places steeped in historical significance. It does not cover prominent cities like Mysuru, Chennai, and Hyderabad, as well as scenic locales like Ooty, Goa, and Kerala, as they need more than a day to tour.

Link in Amazon Store:
https://www.amazon.com/dp/B0CLK58KTB

A Trip to the Wagah Border

The Wagah Border, straddling India and Pakistan near Amritsar and Lahore, is famed for its ceremonial displays by border forces, symbolising hope amidst strained relations. This checkpoint, pivotal for prisoner exchanges, represents a unique reconciliation potential. On festive occasions, friendly exchanges between the forces foster harmony. The book visually explores Chandigarh, Shimla, Amritsar, and the Wagah Border, highlighting their rich cultures and historical importance.

Link in Amazon Store:
https://www.amazon.com/dp/B0CLYTQ6PV

Weekend Getaways from Bengaluru

This guidebook enhances the tourism experience in India, emphasising the country's improved accessibility and facilities that cater to all traveller categories. It explicitly outlines short trips from Bengaluru, covering a mix of destinations accessible by road, rail, and air. The book is a resource for planning 2-, 3-, and 4-day excursions to various South Indian locales and select sites in Maharashtra, featuring popular tourist destinations such as Ooty, Kodaikanal, and Mysuru, as well as revered places of worship like Kukke Subramanya and Dharamsthala. It offers practical travel tips, what to anticipate on journeys and insights into each destination's unique offerings.

Link in Amazon Store: https://www.amazon.com/dp/B0CMNRKWQ9

www.ingramcontent.com/pod-product-compliance
Lightning Source LLC
Chambersburg PA
CBHW052142220526
45471CB00004B/1493